THE FLEA CIRCUS

**How to Break Bad Habits
& Live Effectively**

DR SCOTT ZARCINAS

OTHER BOOKS BY SCOTT ZARCINAS

Non-fiction

Being YOU! (*Your Natural State of Being)
It's Up to YOU!
The Power of YOU!
The Banana Trap

Fiction

Samantha Honeycomb
The Golden Chalice
DeVille's Contract
Ananda
Roadman

THE FLEA CIRCUS

**How to Break Bad Habits
& Live Effectively**

DR SCOTT ZARCINAS

DoctorZed
Publishing
www.doctorzed.com

Copies of this book can be ordered via the author's website at
www.scottzarcinas.com, booksellers or by contacting:

DoctorZed Publishing
10 Vista Ave, Skye,
South Australia 5072
www.doctorzed.com

ISBN: 978-0-6452497-9-8 (hc)
ISBN: 978-0-6452497-8-1 (sc)
ISBN: 978-0-6452497-7-4 (e)

A CiP number is available at the National Library of Australia.

Cover image Vintage Circus Poster © Rompikapo | Dreamstime.com
Cover image Circus Tent © Macrovector | Dreamstime.com

Printed in Australia, UK and USA

DoctorZed Publishing rev. date: 31/10/2023

CONTENTS

For you, who desires to become that which you are capable of being.

AND

Leonie McKeon
Who believed in me and what I am tyring to achieve.

WELCOME!

HELLO AND WELCOME. I'd like to congratulate you on taking this step to unlock the true potential of your life and embark on the process of personal growth.

As with my other books, this guidebook is an alternative to quick-fix, result-driven recipes for 'success' in life. It is a process of knowing yourself better, a process of *how* to think, not a manual of what to think.

And because it is a process it is something that will continue throughout your life. There is no end to the process of personal growth—but what you will find is that the process will help you breakthrough your barriers and transcend your limits.

The process, therefore, means dedication, focus, and constant work on your behalf, and to keep persisting with the process of transformation into the person you are capable of becoming.

It is my hope and intent to now help empower you to the abundance and fullness that life has to offer using the specific knowledge of *The Flea Circus*.

Dr. Scott Zarcinas
2023

A WORD OF ENCOURAGEMENT

THIS GUIDEBOOK IS not a magic wand that will make all your problems disappear. Nor is it a magic carpet that will take you to a place far from your worries and concerns.

On the contrary, this guidebook will cause you to reflect on your issues and encourage you to move past them.

But you are not without help.

This book will equip you with the necessary tools to help you break through your barriers and to become the person you are capable of being.

As the parable says:

> *Give a man a fish,*
> *You feed him for a day.*
> *Teach a man how to fish,*
> *You feed him for a lifetime.*

THE FLEA CIRCUS

In days gone by, a flea circus was a circus sideshow attraction in which fleas were trained to perform miniature circus acts, keeping patrons amused until the main event.

Flea trainers trained the fleas to kick miniature balls, pull small carts, even rotate miniature Ferris wheels.

Fleas, though, have the incredible ability to leap eighty times their own height. This is the equivalent of a six-foot human jumping four hundred and eighty feet into the air, or over a forty-eight-storey building. However, fleas can be trained to jump only a few inches high. But how?

A flea trainer does this with a simple deception, by placing an upended glass or cup over the fleas. When the fleas try to jump, they hit a ceiling, which is the bottom of the cup.

Over time, the fleas learn they can't jump any higher and are tricked into thinking this is the limit of their capabilities.

When the cup is removed, however, the fleas don't return to their normal leaping abilities. Rather, they are fettered by their training and continue to leap as if the glass or cup was still above them.

Likewise, your mind places a virtual ceiling of thoughts, emotions and beliefs above you, causing you to live within self-prescribed limitations. Your mind tricks you into believing that you're not capable of doing more or being more effective.

The flea circus is therefore a great metaphor for how your mind can limit your full potential and minimise your effectiveness—*it puts an invisible barrier to your hopes and dreams that only you can remove.*

There is a quote by Bruce Lee that sums this up beautifully, and in fact is the glue that binds all the words and sentences in this book together:

> *If you always put a limit on everything you do, physical or anything else, it will spread into your work and into your life. There are no limits. There are only plateaus and you must not stay there, you must go beyond them.*

But there is no need to put limitations on yourself any longer. For the rest of this guidebook, we will discuss how to break through your barriers and transcend your limits.

This is how you avoid being just another flea in the flea circus.

AN INTRODUCTION TO SELF-LEADERSHIP

'All limits are self-imposed.'

Icarus

It has been said that we overestimate what we can achieve in a day, and underestimate what we can achieve in a lifetime.

But when we overestimate what we can do in the limited number of hours we have during the day, we become overwhelmed. There's simply too much to do in too little time. We feel inundated. We feel time-pressured. We feel like throwing our hands in the air and giving up.

Overwhelm over a long period of time, however, can lead to bigger problems like chronic stress, ingrained feelings of failure, and long-term dissatisfaction with life, which, unfortunately, is a common experience for a lot of people.

Unable to find a solution to this, we work harder and harder, thinking that if we just keep doing what we've done we will eventually get to where we want.

Little do we realise that doing the same thing over and over only gets the same result. Which is usually nowhere, struggling to 'be someone' or 'get somewhere'. Feeling more and more overwhelmed because we are running and running and running like hamsters on a wheel, trying to achieve more than we are physically capable of doing, and end up staying exactly where we are.

Worse, we end the day physically tired and mentally exhausted, dreading the next day because the work we didn't complete today will pile onto the workload for tomorrow.

"Things will only get worse before they get worse," we say to ourselves.

Overloaded, we lurch from day to day, just managing to get by, wondering if it's ever going to end. Wondering if we are ever going to get respite and much-needed rest. Wondering how the heck we ever got ourselves into this situation in the first place.

So we are overcome with feelings of powerlessness and futility. We feel stuck in a rut, we feel stagnant, we feel as though we are unable to get over the hump, unable to live the life we have always wanted and hoped for.

For all our hard work and efforts, all we have succeeded in doing is dig ourselves into a hole in the cemetery of lost dreams.

"Why bother?" we ask ourselves. "It doesn't matter how hard I work, I still can't get ahead. There's no point."

This mindset is self-defeating because it puts limits on who you think you are and what you believe you can achieve. Worse, this mindset is a white flag, a surrender to life, an acceptance of mediocrity and averageness.

Which, on the surface might seem okay and better than most of the world who live in poverty and struggle every day for the basics of life, but this mindset can only lead to one end—to stagnation and a smothering of the human spirit.

So we start believing that this is as good as it gets. We give up striving for anything we once hoped of doing. We settle for less and justify our capitulation by claiming there was nothing more that could have been done. It's just the way it is.

We then park the bus and stop chasing the dream. We stop listening to our hopes and desires, we poison our passions with counter-reasoning and logic (aka scepticism), and we learn to live without hope and learn to get comfortable with nagging frustration. We lose the joy of life. We become the living dead.

What happens next, though, is disastrous: we deliberately and fearfully curtail our plans for the future, fully undermining what we are truly capable of achieving.

Then we teach our children to do the same thing, and the sins of the father are passed onto the child.

We teach them to make the same mistakes we made. We teach them to put up with their lot and to not complain about it. This becomes our legacy, a legacy of self-defeat.

You might be thinking that this assumption is a little over the top and is simply not true because there are things beyond our control that impact what we can and cannot do in our lives.

You might be thinking that you had no choice into which socioeconomic situation you were born, or for that matter your gender, race, or country. These factors impact your opportunity for change and are completely beyond your sphere of influence.

But I want you to think about what really stops you from achieving? I want you to think about what really prevents you from fulfilling your true potential? What really limits your success?

For most, it isn't anything to do with your socioeconomic situation, your gender, race, or country of birth. In truth, it's something you have complete and total control over:

How you think!

Why? Because the focus of your thoughts determines your perspective, and therefore what you perceive.

In other words, that upon which you place your attention determines your experience—how you focus determines your perception of 'what is', which becomes your reality.

As the Budha said:

With your thoughts you create your world.

Therefore, if you are not living the life you want, if you are not achieving the results you wished and hoped for, if you are unable to transition from ineffectiveness to effectiveness, you need to refine how you focus and how you think.

You need to take control of your mind and take responsibility for what you focus your attention on. Failure to do so will inevitably lead to dysfunctional thoughts, reactive emotions, and self-limiting behaviours—perfect ingredients for stagnation, non-achievement, and perpetual failure.

You can't solve a problem with the same thinking that created it, as Einstein said. The answer, therefore, isn't to work harder at doing the same things that haven't elevated you to where you want to go. Rather, it is to work *smarter*.

You need to work less on your external world, and to work more on your internal world. You need to ready yourself and work on your mind before you work on your tasks.

As the saying goes:

> *Get yourself right first, and everything else will fall into place.*

But that is the essential point: we must first get ourselves right.

A builder gets the foundation right before he builds the walls of the house. A doctor educates herself before treating her first patient. A sailor mends his sails before venturing out to sea.

To paraphrase Abraham Lincoln:

> *Give me six hours to chop down a tree and I will spend the first four sharpening the blade.*

You might well be the strongest lumberjack in the woods, but if your tools are blunt then you are at a severe disadvantage.

This is the essence of self-leadership, to spend more time on sharpening your blade—*your mind*—than on the tasks at hand.

To this point, there are 4 main factors on which to focus and sharpen:

1. Who do you want to be?
2. What do you want to do?
3. Why do you want to do it?
4. How do you want to do it?

As a general rule, unfortunately, most people lack the clarity of who they want to be and what they really want to achieve.

The problem is that they are so caught up in the constant overwhelm and stresses of life that they have become distracted and have lost focus on who they are and want to be.

They have become so caught up in the busyness of their lives that they have forgotten the most important thing they need to do—to work *on* their life.

So they fall back into the same old habits of doing more, running faster, working longer, but all they are doing is trying to chop down a tree with a blunt blade.

Those who are effective self-leaders—those that I call Life Leaders—understand this. They understand that their success is directly related to how they focus and think.

They therefore work hard to sharpen their mindset. To grind away any mental barriers and psychological limitations, especially any thoughts, emotions, words, or actions that limit who they are and want to be.

Good self-leadership, therefore, is essential if you want to become the person you are capable of being and want to live the life you always dreamed.

THE LIFE LEADERSHIP COMPASS

I'd like to now introduce the Life Leadership Compass. This compass is a visual representation of the self-leadership habits you'll need to develop to become more effective—your Who, What, Why, How—which we will be undertaking henceforth.

You can use the Life Leadership Compass to identify the areas on which you need to work and improve, as well as strengthening the areas you are already good at.

Think of the Life Leadership Compass not as a set series of rules to follow, rather as a guide with which you can tailor to your own needs.

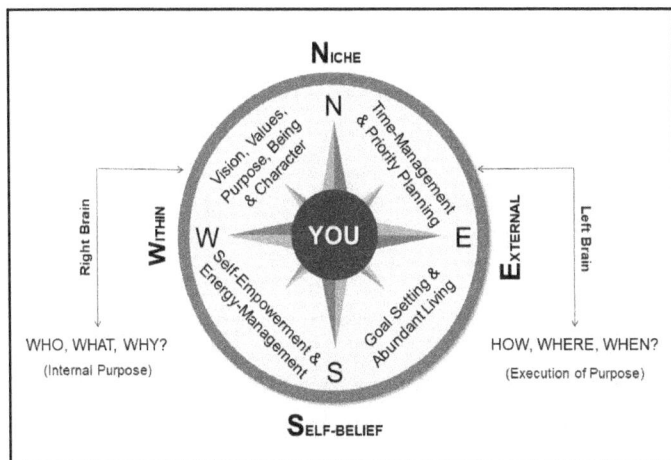

FIGURE 1: The Life Leadership Compass

At the centre of the Life Leadership Compass is you. Everything in your life begins and ends with you, including who you want to be and doing what you want to do.

You are the central axis upon which pivots everything you want to become and everything you want to achieve. If you are not the centre of your own life, then who is?

Clarity of who you are—your 'I am'—is therefore your direction finder; without it, you are likely to wander around and around in circles trying to find yourself, lost and not knowing which way to go.

Clarity of who you are is *the* essential factor in being effective because it defines who you want to be, what you want to do, and why you want to do it—your inner purpose.

It also defines how you do what you want to do, and where and when you want to do it—the execution of your purpose.

Your 'Niche' is your true north. It's that one place in this world where you can express your true potential and become the person you are capable of becoming.

Your 'Niche' is where you find your passion and your calling. It is where your inner 'being' and outer 'doing' are perfectly aligned. It's where your effectiveness is maximised, even limitless, that place or state where you are truly fulfilled.

Helping to orientate you to your true north, or 'Niche', is your vision of who you are, the values and principles by which you live, and your life purpose.

It also includes the intentional expression of your natural state of being,[1] which is the essence of who you really are—

---

[1] Read *Being YOU! Awaken to the Abundance of Your Natural State of Being*, Scott Zarcinas MD, DoctorZed Publishing, 2023

joy, security, acceptance, peace, and freedom—and the lifelong development of strong character traits.

Identifying your vision, values, and purpose engages that part of your right brain responsible for creativity and imagination —essential for developing good self-management habits.

Other techniques and activities like time-management, goal-setting, and priority planning engage that part of your left brain responsible for reasoning and logic, which assist the successful execution of your goals (your how, where, when).

Self-belief is your south or 'S' compass point. Self-belief is your driving force, from which springs your enthusiasm, confidence, and motivation to take action.

Self-belief is one half of the equation for what I call 'Power Consciousness'. Without self-belief, you are like a vehicle without fuel: everything has stalled and you can't move forward.

Helping you to develop a stronger sense of self-belief are right-brain self-empowerment activities and techniques that are designed to boost positive self-talk and a positive self-image, even boost your energy stocks.

Other left-brain activities and techniques, such as goal-setting, can boost yourself-belief through planning specific and realistic pathways to get to where you want to go.

These Life Leadership Compass strategies and habits will be discussed in the following chapters in order to increase your effectiveness through better self-management.

For now, though, review *Figure 1: The Life Leadership Compass*, and reflect on these questions:

> Q: What areas of the Life Leadership Compass are you already doing well in your personal life and professional work?

> Q: What areas of the Life Leadership Compass do you feel you need to strengthen or focus on?

PART I

THE

EFFECTIVENESS

EQUATION

1 CHALLENGES TO YOUR EFFECTIVENESS

'Efficiency is doing things right. Effectiveness is doing the right things.'

Peter Drucker

YOUR EFFECTIVENESS TODAY is the direct result of your past choices. In other words, your self-leadership. It is the direct consequence of the decisions you made yesterday, last week, last month, last year, even decades ago.

In a sense, any measure of success—health, wealth, happiness, well-being, relationships—is a direct consequence of how effective you have been up until this moment in time.

> *Effectiveness is the degree to which you are able to produce a desired result.*

That is, effectiveness is the degree to which you are able to produce a desired *effect*. When you can cause an intended effect, you are effective.

You have most probably heard of Einstein's famous equation, $E = MC^2$, where E is energy, M is mass, and C is the speed of light (which is the fastest thing in the universe at nearly 300,000,000 metres per second).

Likewise, your professional and personal effectiveness can also be expressed as a formula, whereby your effectiveness is the product of your mental, emotional, and physical ability to cause an intended outcome or result.

I've adapted Einstein's equation to take into account these factors and produced an equation that you can follow to supercharge your effectiveness:

$$E = MC^2 \text{ (or } E = M \times C_1 \times C_2 \text{)}$$

In this new equation, E is effectiveness, M is mindset, C_1 is capability, and C_2 is capacity.

> *Your mindset, capability, and capacity are the three*
> *essential or dependent variables that determine your*
> *overall level of effectiveness.*

Your mindset (M) is your attitude, especially in respect to your attitude to yourself, your physical, mental, and emotional energy levels, and your time. We will begin discussing mindset in just a moment in *Common Challenges to Effectiveness*.

Your capability (C_1) is your power or ability to do something. It is the extent of your ability to fulfill a need or requirement. When you are capable, the chance of successfully completing an intended task is high. When you have low capability, or you are somewhat incapable, the chance of failure is high.

Where capability has a qualitative aspect to it, your capacity (C_2) has a quantitative aspect to it. Capacity is measured in volume, and like a cup or a bucket it refers to how much you can 'hold'. If your physical, mental, and emotional capacity is high, you are able to handle a lot. If your physical, mental, and emotional capacity is low, you cannot handle as much.

Therefore, according to The Effectiveness Equation, along with the right mindset, the higher your capability and the higher your capacity, the higher your personal and professional effectiveness will be.

Anything that boosts your capability and capacity will boost your effectiveness. Anything that limits or diminishes your capability and capacity will limit or diminish your effectiveness.

These three variables—mindset, capability, capacity— are therefore what we will be focusing on and discussing throughout this guidebook to supercharge your effectiveness.

But if you want to pare effectiveness down to one word, that word would be *choice*.

The choices you make are powerful because they either boost your mindset, capability, and capacity, or they put limits on them. Your choices either confine you like a flea in a flea circus, or they release you. You choose your limits.

Your present level of effectiveness is thus a reflection of the choices you have made till now, and your future level of effectiveness will be a reflection of the choices you make from this moment forward.

Effectiveness really is about choice.

When you consider the current issues you face, and trace them back to the choices you have made, you will uncover the vital link between your thoughts and the experiences that followed.

> *You will also see the importance of shifting the focus of your attention if you want to manifest a different experience.*

For example, seeing the glass half-full results in a different life experience—physical, mental, emotional, and spiritual— than seeing the glass half-empty.

But it's just a choice. A choice of where to shift the focus of your attention.

This shift in focus is a mindshift challenge I call 'The Life Leadership Imperative'. It has the power to not only change your life for the better, but also that of your family, your friends, your community, the entire planet.

The contemporary definition of insanity is to do the same thing over and over again and expect a different result. The path to your prosperous future, therefore, is created by thinking differently—by thinking like a Life Leader.

As a Life Leader, you must be true to yourself and be brave to express the real you. You must focus on who you really are and *live it*. In doing so, you will discover your inner power.

And those with inner power are effective in everything they do and in everything they are. They are effective Life Leaders.

COMMON CHALLENGES TO EFFECTIVENESS

What follows in this guidebook is the vital role your thoughts, emotions, and beliefs have in determining your effectiveness.

> *What stands between you and your true potential is the way you think.*

Think about that. The bridge from where you are now to where you want to be is how well you use your thinking apparatus—your mind.

A big part of how you think includes your perspective, how you see the world, your awareness of what is, which is influenced by your frame of reference—your *mindset orientation*.

Your mindset orientation—perspective—creates the context with which you view yourself and your interaction with the events happening around you. That is, how you perceive your place in the world.

Your perspective is your point of view, and your point of view can change depending on how you choose to position yourself in relation to the world around you. When your orientation changes, your perspective changes, and thus your point of view changes.

For instance, just as you would when climbing higher up a mountain, once you take a different perspective, you get a different point of view. The higher you ascend, the higher your perspective.

If your perspective hasn't changed for 20 years, if you still have the same point of view in your forties as you did in your twenties, then you haven't moved. You haven't shifted your orientation. You've remained stationary and thus you still see things the same way, from the same angle.

Here are some examples of perspective and mindset orientation:

- Do you see the glass half-full or half-empty?
- Do you see problems in every opportunity, or opportunity in every problem?
- Do you see 101 ways that can go wrong, or 101 ways that can go right?
- Do you see yourself as worthless, or worthy?
- Do you see only ugliness in the world, or do you see the eternal goodness and beauty of Life?
- Do you see your problems as bigger than you, or yourself as bigger than your problems?
- Do you 'want a life', or does Life want you?
- Do you see yourself as a victim or as a victor?
- Do you feel isolated and separated from life and everyone else, or are you connected and one with the Source of Life?
- Do you see yourself as a human being having a spiritual experience, or as a spiritual being having a human experience?

Yet, even a climber's view from the mountain is sometimes obscured by clouds, rain, and mist. So too your perspective can be obscured by your own thoughts, biases, beliefs, and assumptions.

Below is a table of common challenges that can cloud your perspective, and thus limit your ability to build effectiveness.

> Q: Do any of the listed challenges ring true to you? What challenges do you face in being effective, energised, and engaged at home and at work?

COMMON CHALLENGES TO EFFECTIVENESS	
Procrastination.	Perfectionism.
No motivation.	Negative thinking.
Disorganised / time poor.	Too overwhelmed.
Failure to set goals.	Lack of know-how.
Mind fog.	Poor communication.
Exhausted / energy drains.	Lack of purpose / direction.

TABLE 1: Common Challenges to Effectiveness

A vital part of building your effectiveness—inner power—is knowing who and where you are now (mindset orientation) and who you want to be and where you want to go (future vision). You need to have clarity of your current location and clarity of the destination you want to reach. Only then can you have a clear view of the path to get to where you want to go.

You wouldn't board a plane or ferry for three hours not knowing which port you need to depart or your intended destination.

Likewise, your time investment in this book needs to have a departure point and a destination—you need to know where you currently stand and what outcomes you want to achieve.

As Seneca, a Roman poet and stoic philosopher, said:

> *If you do not know to which port you are sailing,*
> *then no wind is helpful.*

Q: With this in mind, what would you specifically like to know or learn in this guidebook about overcoming your challenges to building effectiveness?

Your answer is extremely important because it sets the goal you wish to accomplish. Once you have clarity on what you want to know and learn, you will have direction.

You will have a port to which you want to sail and arrive.

THE PROCESS OF TRANSFORMATION

Let's now talk about 'The Process of Transformation' and how you can use this process to transform your life by establishing better self-leadership habits.

A photon of light exists simultaneously in two states: as a particle (here and now) and as a waveform (pure potential). Likewise, as we are all made of light energy at our core, everybody has two states of existence:

1. The state where we are now—*current* (here and now).
2. The state where we want to be—*desired* (potential).

Whether your current state is meaningful and fulfilled and you want your future desired state to remain the same, or your current state lacks meaning and is unfulfilled and you want your future desired state to be completely different, you still exist in two states—where you are now and where you want to be.

But whatever state you are in currently, the successful arrival at your desired future state requires three things:

1. An effective formula.
2. Effective discipline.
3. Effective habits.

Without these three things, getting to where you want to get to will be due more to good luck than to good process. But successful people don't rely on luck. They may take calculated risks, yet these risks are always backed up by a solid process, rigid discipline, and good habits.

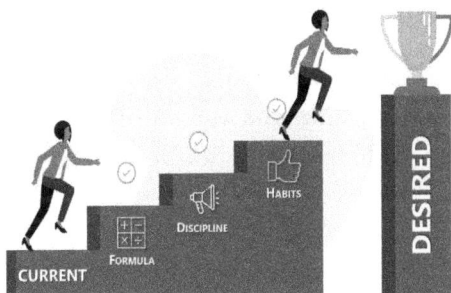

FIGURE 2: The Process of Transformation

Bill Gates, the co-founder of Microsoft and one of the richest men in history, didn't rely on luck for his fortune. In an interview with *Time Magazine* in 2018, he spoke of the importance of having an effective process:

> *If you want to improve something, look for ways to build better systems.*

How Effective Transformation Works

A good example of an effective formula is a diet. If your goal is to lose a specified amount of weight or to eat healthier, then following a nutritional diet is the first thing you need to do.

Your current state is your body's current weight or Body Mass Index (BMI)[2] and overall healthiness. Your desired state is a lower body weight or BMI, or improved healthiness.

To get to your desired state, you need to be disciplined in following your chosen diet. You will face temptations whenever you see an advert for McDonalds or Dominos Pizza, or when you drive past your favourite bakery or patisserie.

But you need to be disciplined. You need to keep in mind your desired outcome and resist any temptation to break your diet.

Once you have established a disciplined diet, this then becomes a new habit[3] and you will find it easier to resist temptation the longer you follow your dietary plan.

This is simply what good self-management looks like, and you know you have reached the level of a new habit when you go to do something differently (for example, eat a pizza, drink alcohol), and it feels 'not you' or awkward.

---

[2] Your BMI is the measure of the amount of muscle, fat and bone in your body, given in kg/m^2. Obesity is defined as a BMI > 30, normal 18.5 - 25, and underweight < 18.5.

[3] Researchers estimate that new habits take 21 days to become established. You can read the neuroscience of why this is so in my book, *It's Up To You! Why Most People Fail to Live the Life they Want and How to Change It*, DoctorZed Publishing, 2019

In time, once you've started following your diet (formula), you are disciplined and resist temptation until a new eating habit has been developed, you will achieve the results you are after.

> *Your results will look after themselves when you look after the process.*

This process, in fact, is the exact self-leadership process you use to build your effectiveness, the master key to success:

-> *Follow a formula. Be disciplined. Make it a habit.*

If you are proactive in doing this, then you remove luck from the equation and you greatly increase the odds of getting to your desired state, which is being highly effective.

The formula we will use throughout this guidebook is The Effectiveness Equation: $E = MC^2$, and we will discuss the many ways you can implement this formula in your day-to-day activities and thus transform your life.

Why Effective Transformation Fails to Happen

Most people, however, fail to achieve the results they want and had hoped for because:

1. They fail to create or find an effective formula.
2. They are not disciplined even if they do find an effective formula.
3. They establish bad habits.

If you don't find an effective formula, then any formula will do. But that means any result will do, and this is no way to build effectiveness or achieve your goals.

If you're not disciplined, if your want is weak and your desire to achieve your goal is lukewarm, then it will be easy to get distracted and be led astray from your plans.

If the habits you have formed are dubious, inconsistent, or even self-destructive, the chances of achieving your goal are severely limited.

Or worse, your situation deteriorates and you end up being worse off than when you started.

> Q: Consider when you had been less successful than what you had hoped. Was it due to any or all of the below?
>
> 1. No effective formula.
> 2. Ill discipline.
> 3. Bad habits.

Take a moment to consider your answers above and whether the outcome would have been more successful if you had followed an effective formula, been more disciplined, or developed better habits.

> Q: Describe how the outcome would have changed, and give your reasons, if you had:
>
> 1. An effective formula.
> 2. Been more disciplined.
> 3. Developed better habits.

Following this process of formula-discipline-habit is essential if your intention is to break through your barriers and become a person of high effectiveness. It is essential because your success will be the result of what process you implement; and the process you choose to implement will inevitably be the result of a positive mental attitude—from the way you *think*.

The opposite is also true. Failure to plan or to follow a formula, being ill-disciplined about that plan, and hanging onto bad habits are essential if you wish to develop *ineffectiveness* and fail in your endeavours.

Failure, therefore, is also a process, and it generally arises from a negative mental attitude—from the way you *think*.

> *How you think will be the difference between being more effective or ineffective.*

How you think will be the difference between being a person of success or a person of failure.

Main Points:

1. Your effectiveness today is the direct result of your past choices.
2. Effectiveness is the degree to which you are able to produce a desired result.
3. The Effectiveness Equation: $E = MC^2$
4. Your mindset (M), capability (C_1), and capacity (C_2) are the three essential or dependent variables that determine your overall level of effectiveness (E).
5. Effectiveness really is about choice.
6. What stands between you and your true potential is the way you think!
7. You have two states of existence—current and desired.
8. Your results will look after themselves when you look after the process: Follow a formula, be disciplined, make it a habit.
9. How you think will be the difference between being more effective or ineffective.

2 CLARITY & PURPOSE

'You only know yourself when you go beyond your limits.'
Paulo Coelho

GETTING CLARITY ON who you are and what you are striving to achieve is vital if you are going to be more effective.

Many people, however, don't have that clarity. They have mind fog, which settles like a thick mist and clouds their vision of who they want to be, what they want to do, as well as which direction they want to be heading.

In short, they are lost. They constantly feel as if they are groping their way through the fog and yearning for a way out. They feel frustrated at the lack of direction in their life. They feel powerless at being unable to change things for the better.

One way to lift the mind fog and get clarity, find direction, and build confidence is to understand who you are being in each area of your life.

Every day you fulfil many roles, many times without realising it: at home, at work, with friends, with family, as a member of your community. You shift seamlessly between your different roles throughout the day, often fulfilling more than one role at a time and most often unconsciously because you've done it so often over the years you don't even have to think about it.

But think about it you must if you truly want to be more effective and successful.

BEING & DOING: THE 7 LIFE SEGMENTS

As a general rule, the many things you do and the many roles you have on a day-to-day basis can be divided into 7 Life Segments:

1. Family & Relationships
2. Career & Work
3. Money & Finances
4. Health & Wellbeing
5. Learning & Education
6. Fun & Adventure
7. Spirituality & Ethics (or Morals & Religion)

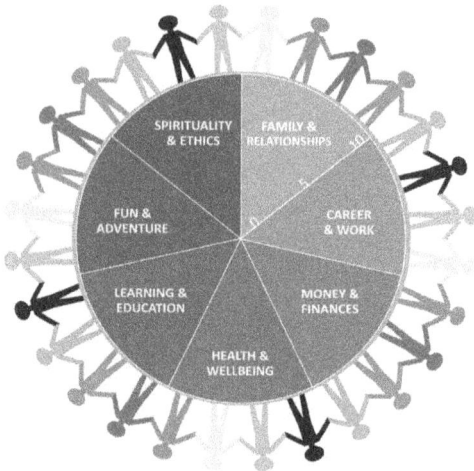

FIGURE 3: The 7 Life Segments

Although there are others, these 7 Life Segments encompass the main areas on which you can focus and set goals to achieve throughout your life.

> Q: Rate each of your 7 Life Segments on a scale of 0-10 (where 0 is lowest and 10 is highest).

For instance, you might rate Career & Work as 8, Learning & Education as 6, Family & Relationships as 10, and so forth. You might even rate each Life Segment equally. You might discover that one Life Segment rates well above all the others. Another might rate well below all the others.

There is no right or wrong in this exercise. What's important isn't the value of each Life Segment per se, rather the importance lies in the value of each Life Segment in relation to the other Life Segments.

> Q: Now rank each of your 7 Life Segments in order of importance 1-7 and state your reasons.

Ranking your Life Segments assigns their level of importance to you, and the rating value you assigned to each Life Segment will help you to rank them in order of importance. Generally speaking, the higher the rating the higher the ranking.

For instance, Money & Finances might rank No. 1, Fun & Adventure No. 2, Health & Wellbeing No. 3, and so forth. If you have rated two or more Life Segments equally, you will need to make a subjective decision as to which one ranks higher in importance and value to you.

Q: Consider what you currently do or want to do in each of your 7 Life Segments. What is essential or central to what you are *doing* in each segment?

For instance, in the Life Segment of Family & Relationships you probably have multiple roles, such as brother/sister/sibling, mother/father/parent, husband/wife/partner, grandparent/uncle/aunt/cousin, friend/colleague/teammate, and so forth.

Now consider what is central to what you do in your roles within this Life Segment? For example, as a friend your central role is to be supportive, to be a shoulder to cry on, to help out, to be there for your friends in times of need.

If you are a parent, your central role is to provide and protect. You provide for the needs of your children, and you provide shelter and protection for them.

You also heal and teach your children. You heal them when they hurt themselves, and you care for them when they are unwell. You also teach them family values and your cultural history. You teach them about money, proper behaviour and respect, and the importance of being kind to others. You teach them to love themselves.

Yet although doing is different from being, they are often confused as the same thing. For instance, how often have you heard someone say, "You are what you do!"?

Which is nonesense, of course:

You cannot do without being, but you can be without doing.

Just because you might 'do' some teaching of your children doesn't mean you are a teacher. Rather, you are being a parent who is doing some teaching.

Likewise, when younger siblings are left in the care of their older sister while their parents return home from work, the older sister doesn't suddenly become her younger siblings' parent because she's temporarily taken the responsibility of looking after the children. She remains the older sister albeit 'doing' some parenting.

The parent doing some teaching, and the older sister doing some parenting, are not confusing their current actions with who they are. They are able to differentiate what they are doing from who they are being.

Those who confuse doing with being, however, simply have a case of mistaken identity: they think they are human doings, not human beings.

But to think this way is severely self-limiting, which this guidebook aims to address. To identify only with what you are doing externalises yourself to that thing you are doing.

The problem, and self-limiting aspect of this externalisation of identity, is that when you stop doing that thing you are doing, your identity dies with it.

This would be extremely disconcerting if it were true. But can you really stop being who you are at any point during this lifetime? Is your beingness that fragile and dependent on external factors?

Of course not. If, for some reason, as a parent you are unable to provide for your children or protect them, it would be nonsensical to say that you are no longer a parent. If you are unable for whatever reason to be supportive to your friends, it doesn't mean that you are no longer a friend.

You are not a parent or friend because of what you do, you are a parent and friend because of who you are in your heart, who you are in spirit.

First you *are* a parent or friend, then you *act* as a parent or friend. You don't act as a parent or friend and then become a parent or friend. Being a parent or friend precedes doing anything that a parent or friend does.

Who you are is primary. What you do is secondary.

> *Who you are being is the cause, and what you are doing is the effect.*

This is why 'You' are the hub of your Life Leadership Compass and not what you do.

> Q: Now consider your roles and who you are being in each of your 7 Life Segments. What is essential or central to who you are *being* in each segment?

In other words, what is the core value that underpins who you are in each Life Segment? What is the essence of who you are (or want to be) that you are expressing?

As a friend, your core value or essence is loyalty and fidelity, which is expressed through faithfulness and continuing support to your friends. It implies trust, honesty, reliability.

As a parent, your core value or essence is most probably love and nurture. Love and nurture is expressed through your desire for your children to be healthy and to grow into the adult they are capable of becoming.

Your loving and nurturing essence is expressed through loving and nurturing actions. It is imbued in everything you think, say, feel, and do for the benefit of your children. Which is the important distinction between being and doing, cause and effect:

> *What you do is imbued with the essence of your being—who you are is how you act.*

When you squeeze an orange, you get orange juice. When you squeeze a lemon, you get lemon juice. The essence in sweetness and sourness, therefore, is not in the juice itself but in where it has come from.

If you are being angry, you will think angry thoughts, and you will ultimately act with anger. If you are being hateful, you will think hateful thoughts, and you will ultimately act with hatred.

If you are being resentful, you will think resentful thoughts, and you will ultimately act with resentment.

However, if you are being kind, you will think kind thoughts, and you will ultimately act with kindness. If you are being truthful, you will think truthful thoughts, and you will ultimately act with honesty. If you are being loving, you will think loving thoughts, and you will ultimately act with love.

This, then, is the essence of high effectiveness:

> *Elevate who you are being and you elevate what you do.*

In other words, how effective you are in this moment is a direct result of who you are being in this moment. So, if becoming more effective is a priority for you, then who you are being must become your top priority.

Prioritising being before doing must become your focus.

YOUR PURPOSE: THE RETAINED MODEL

Your purpose is your reason for doing what you do and how you do it. It's the 'why' you do what you say you will do, your 'why' for striving to achieve what you want to achieve. In simple terms, it's your reason for getting out of bed in the morning.

For a lot of people, the reason they get out of bed is to earn money so they can pay the bills and put food on the table. For others, it's to go to school or university to get an education. Some actually don't know why they get out of bed and so spend the rest of the day in a state of despair and annoyance.

These people are unmotivated and disengaged with what they are doing, spending most of the day on autopilot and wishing they were somewhere else. In fact, they are so unmotivated that getting out of bed is quite possibly the hardest thing they have to do during the day.

It's safe to say that these people rank low on the scale of effectiveness. Unfortunately, they are not alone. In fact, they have many friends. A Galllup Poll in 2017 in the USA suggested that at any one point up to 85% of employees are disengaged at work.

This means that if you walk into any office at any time of the workday, five out of every six staff in the building are not engaged with the work they are doing. They are procrastinating, doing something other than the task at hand, deliberately avoiding work, gossiping, or they are distracted with other things. The cost of this loss of productivity to the US economy is estimated at US$550 billion per year.[4]

Disengagement at work usually happens when an employee is not aligned with the company's core values. There is conflict between what the employee believes in and wants, and what the company believes in and wants. It behooves the company, therefore, to get to know its employees and understand what they believe in or want during their employment, and vice versa.

Generally speaking, most employees seek one or more of these following things from their place of employment: remuneration, education, trust, appreciation, involvement, new opportunities, empowerment, and motive.

---

[4] *The Engaged Institute, 2017*

Each of these eight factors are a kind of personalised purpose for each employee to get out of bed and go to work. I call this group of eight factors 'The RETAINED Model™', and employers would benefit from understanding each employee and what motivates them to come to work each day.

It would also benefit each employee to know why they continue to get up and go to work, day in, day out, even for their own well-being and happiness.

FIGURE 4:   The RETAINED Model™

The RETAINED Model™

R: Remuneration

Staff and employees want to be paid for what they do, unless they are volunteers who are happy to work for nothing. They want fair remuneration for the work they perform. They have bills to pay, they have food to put on the table, they have a roof to keep over their heads, as well as many other outgoings that need to be paid for.

Getting paid and having a regular paycheck is therefore important. But, surprisingly, it isn't the number one reason people go to work.

> Q: Consider when you have been underpaid or you received inadequate remuneration for the work you have done. How did it make you feel? What did you do about it?

E: Education

Being trained and educated on the job is also important, but again it isn't the number one reason staff turn up for work. Saying that, staff do value in-house training and do want to upskill in order to improve their CV, to raise their level of expertise, to become better and more efficient at what they do, and to even push for a promotion.

Imagine working in a job where there was no opportunity for learning, training, or being educated in new and improved ways to do your job. Imagine there being no scope for professional development or self-improvement. Imagine being kept at the same level of knowledge as you did on the first day you walked through the door of your new job years ago.

I imagine it would be severely depressing and demotivating.

> Q: Consider when you have not received proper training or education to do the work you've been asked to perform. How did it make you feel? What did you do about it?

T: Trust

The glue that holds all relationships together is trust.

Your relationship with yourself (do you trust you?). Your relationship with your partner, siblings, children, parents, and other members of your family. Your relationship with your friends. Your relationship with your boss or colleagues.

When trust disappears, the relationship weakens because the bond holding it together has dissolved. Just think of what happens to a marriage when neither partner trusts the other.

This is also true in your workplace. When trust between you and your employer, co-workers, clients, or business partners is fragile or non-existent, then the relationship you have with these people is just as fragile or non-existent and can lead to the business equivalent of a marital breakdown.

They don't trust you, and you don't trust them. This is not a recipe for productivity and effectiveness. It is more a recipe for disharmony and disaster. Distrust in the workplace is curtailing, both for you and for them, and it is just as damaging as any marital distrust.

But on the other hand, a relationship built and maintained on trust will thrive and grow stronger. Whether personal or professional, a trusting relationship is uplifting, positively reinforcing, and mutually beneficial.

This also includes the relationship you have with yourself. You will be so much more effective in everything you want to become, and everything you want to do personally and professionally, when you have a positive relationship with yourself based on trust (see *Trust Thyself*, Chapter 9).

> Q: Consider when you have not trusted your co-workers or your boss, or you were not trusted by them. How did it make you feel? What did you do about it?

A: Appreciation

But trust, although vitally important to all your relationships at home and at work, is still not the number one motivational driver for employees.

Appreciation is.

Business coaches tell us that the main reason people leave their jobs is not because of the work, it's because of the boss.

There are many reasons staff members decide they can no longer work under their leadership or managerial team and seek employment elsewhere: micro-management, inappropriate behaviour, exclusion, distrust, personality issues, constant disapproval, clash of values, sexism.

But one of the main reasons is the lack of appreciation. When we feel constantly underappreciated, we feel disrespected, we feel unwanted, we feel undervalued, we feel surplus to requirements.

We feel as if we are just a number. Just another cog in the machine. We feel as if our presence is no longer needed, and that we can easily be replaced.

But when we feel appreciated, even if it's just a simple "Thank you", we feel respected, we feel valued, we feel needed. We feel as if we are valuable and necessary to the team or organisation, and that our absence will be sorely missed. We feel part of something much bigger than ourselves.

People don't care how much you know until they know how much you care, as they say. So one of the great traits of great leaders is that they care about their staff and fellow co-workers. Conversely, one of the worst traits of poor leaders is that they only care about themselves.

You can't show that you care for someone else if you don't show how much you appreciate them. All it takes is a simple two-word sentence: "Thank you."

It really is that powerful.

Employees, or anyone for that matter, who feel deeply appreciated by their bosses and fellow co-workers feel a deep sense of inner self-worth. Worth is wealth. So inner worth is inner wealth, and that inner wealth is felt and expressed as happiness, well-being, confidence, resilience, assuredness, inner peace, and self-belief.

All the elements of a successful and effective life.

> Q: Consider when you did not receive appreciation or thanks for the work you've been asked to perform. How did it make you feel? What did you do about it?

I: Involved

Similar to feeling appreciated and cared for is the feeling of being included by fellow colleagues or bosses in decision-making and team get-togethers.

As human beings, one of our most innate needs is to belong and to be accepted by others. Birds of a feather flock together for a reason. Which is why employee involvement and inclusion is so important to their well-being and happiness.

One sure way to make others feel unwanted and un-needed, however, is to exclude and isolate them. Exclusion eats at the heart of who we are as human beings. We are social beings, and the feeling of isolation can be devastating to our mental, physical, emotional, and spiritual health.

There's a reason one of the worst punishments anyone can endure is to be incarcerated in solitary confinement. It's also the reason that lockdowns during the COVID-19 pandemic were so devastating to those living alone, especially the elderly.

It's just common sense that happy staff who feel involved and included are more likely to be more productive, more effective, and have more impact and influence in their work environment than those who feel excluded and unwanted.

> Q: Consider when you were excluded from decision-making or not included in team events or gatherings. How did it make you feel? What did you do about it?

N: New Opportunities

On the one hand, although we as human beings crave safety and security and are wary of constant change and anything that threatens our way of life, we also crave freshness and newness.

When we are growing, we feel alive and energetic. Growth is the natural order of things: all life grows and expands. It's our nature.

So we don't like things to stagnate and inhibit our natural tendency to grow. We don't like humdrum. We don't like staleness. We don't like things to stay the same for too long for fear of getting bored.

This is just as relevant in our work and career. We like things to move forward. We like to see progress. We like to feel as if we are moving ahead and climbing the organisational ladder.

We certainly don't want to remain an intern for the whole of our career. We don't want to remain in the classroom. We don't want to remain subordinate and stuck in a role that has no potential for promotion or scope for career advancement.

Which is why one of the main attractions for new employees is the provision of an established career pathway in an organisation and the guarantee of new opportunities to advance and progress through a company hierarchy.

> Q: Consider when promotional opportunities were denied to you, or when career advancement was blocked to you. How did it make you feel? What did you do about it?

E: Empowered

We also like being empowered, to have the ability to do the things we want to do, to have free will, to have self-determination, to have the power to choose the direction our lives take.

The opposite of being empowered is being disempowered. This we don't like. We don't like limitations being placed upon us, or being told what to do. We don't like our freedom being taken away from us. We don't like organisations, religions, governments, corporations, institutions, or community lobbies telling us what to think and how to behave.

But this gets tricky when we sign a contract and go to work for somebody else. Part of holding down a job is to agree to forgo certain freedoms in exchange for an annual salary. Like when and where we can work or take our holidays. Who we work with and sit next to in the office. What we can say to co-workers and clients. How we can dress and present ourselves.

It's really not that much different than going to school. The only difference is that we get paid to suffer this ritual disempowerment.

Even if we rise to the top of the organisational hierarchyy, we are still bound by that organisation's code of conduct. If not more so, because now we are the face of the business and are duty-bound to uphold that code of conduct to the letter.

No wonder so many people crave retirement; it's the only chance they have to break the shackles and regain their freedom.

Yet there is a way to nullify these feelings of disempowerment, whether at home or at work, and that's to accept responsibility.

Responsibility unlocks empowerment. How?

> *Because when you take responsibility for an outcome or an effect, you automatically take responsibility for the process or the cause of that outcome or effect.*

Responsibility for the process or the cause means decision-making. It means deciding between options. It means making choices.

Choice implies power. The power to choose is therefore empowering. The more you choose, the more empowered you are. That's how responsibility unlocks empowerment, through the free will to choose.

So if you want to help your children grow their inner power, give them responsibility. Give them the power to choose. Empower them with the freedom of choice.

If you want to give other co-workers or staff the gift of empowerment, give them responsibility. Give them the power to choose. Empower them with the freedom of choice.

If you want to rediscover your own inner power, give yourself responsibility. Give yourself the power to choose. Empower yourself with the freedom of choice.

> Q: Consider when the freedom to choose was denied to you, or when responsibility was withheld from you. How did it make you feel? What did you do about it?

D: Driven & Motivated

For centuries leaders and managers have devised ways to motivate their subordinates and get the most out of them. More often than not, they've used the carrot or the stick.

The carrots have usually been one or more of the seven factors we've just been discussing: money, training, promotional opportunities, leadership roles, project responsibilities, and so forth. Lately, work-life balance, flexible hours, remote work, health insurance, and increased holidays have been used to entice staff to an organisation or retain their employment.

The sticks, on the other hand, have usually been some sort of punishment, or the threat of some kind of recrimination.

For instance, the Roman military used a disciplinary measure known as 'decimation', which is derived from the Latin term 'decimatio', and refers to the removal of a tenth. This involved the execution of every tenth member within a given group.

Senior commanders resorted to this practice to address serious transgressions committed by their units, such as acts of cowardice, mutiny, desertion, and insubordination. Additionally, it was used as a means of quelling unrest among rebellious legions.

This is an extreme example of how to manage large numbers of people and motivate them to perform as they've been asked. Today, leaders are more likely to use threats of dismissal, financial penalties, demotion, reassignment, and even legal action as means of managing and controlling their team.

But bribery and coercion can only work so far. External inducements and threats of punishment have limitations and do not last. Someone else or some other organisation can always offer a bigger carrot. People will always rise up and rebel against ongoing threats or perceived injustice.

A more long-term solution is to get to the hearts and minds of those you wish to motivate. This requires inspiration. People must feel inspired to give their time and devotion to a cause. They must feel inspired to work for something greater than themselves.

Winston Churchill knew this. His grit and his determination to 'never, never, never surrender' galvanised the whole of the United Kingdom to withstand the Nazi invasion and eventually triumph over them.

John F. Kennedy inspired his country to become the first nation to reach the moon when he gave his famous 'We choose to go to the Moon' speech in 1962 and set the mission for the USA to send a man to the moon and return him home safely before the end of the decade.

Today, businesses, institutions, organisations, and corporations are using similar mission-like statements to galvanise their staff and motivate them to work for a greater cause.

For instance, the United Nations charter states that its purpose is to maintain international peace and security, develop friendly relations among nations, achieve international cooperation, and serve as a centre for harmonising the actions of nations.

Even the TV and movie industry knows about the power of having a clear mission. In the TV series and movies of *Star Trek*, the mission of Captain Kirk and the crew of the *USS Enterprise* is:

> *To explore strange new worlds. To seek out new life and new civilisations. To boldly go where no man has gone before.*

Famous individuals too have made known and implemented their personal mission during their time here on Earth:

- Maya Angelou: "My mission in life is not merely to survive, but to thrive; and to do so with some passion, some compassion, some humour, and some style."
- Oprah Winfrey: "To be a teacher. And to be known for inspiring my students to be more than they thought they could be."
- Mahatma Gandhi: "I shall not fear anyone on Earth. I shall fear only God. I shall not bear ill will toward anyone. I shall not submit to injustice from anyone. I shall conquer untruth by truth. And in resisting untruth, I shall put up with all suffering."
- Walt Disney: "To make people happy."

One of the most inspiring mission statements I've found is the mission statement of SpaceX: "To revolutionise space technology, with the ultimate goal of enabling people to live on other planets." In other words:

> *To help humanity become an interplanetary species.*

I mean, wow! Sign me up!

Can you imagine going to work every day and your job is to help humanity become an interplanetary species?

How much motivation would you need to do your job? I'd be jumping out of bed at the crack of dawn every morning and racing out the door to get to work. Even if my job was to clean the toilets and mop the floors, I'd know that I was doing my bit to help humanity boldly go where it had never gone before. I couldn't think of anything more inspiring or more fulfilling.

That's the role of leadership, to inspire and motivate others with clear vision and purpose.

When a leader can give her people—staff, team, community, nation, family—a clear vision of what she wants to achieve and where she wants to go, then she will get buy-in from those people because they will know the 'why' of what they are being asked to do and they will be driven and motivated to help her achieve that vision.

That's also your role, to inspire and motivate yourself with clear vision and purpose.

When you as a self-leader can give yourself a clear vision of who you want to be, what you want to achieve, and where you want to go, you will 'buy in' to your vision because you will know the 'why' of what you are here to do in this lifetime and you will be driven and motivated to achieve that vision.

That vision is also best kept as simplified as possible. The less complicated the better. A precise, 1-sentence mission statement is far more effective and has far more impact than an overly complicated and vaguely written one.

For instance, my personal mission statement, inspired by the mission statement of SpaceX, is this:

To help humanity become an awakened species.

This statement reflects my commitment to serve the continuous advancement and development of all humankind, to help humanity transform into what we are truly capable of becoming: a peaceful, loving, joyous, free, limitless species where all may have life and have it abundantly.

This statement keeps me driven and motivated to keep writing my books. It keeps me motivated to keep doing what I need to do to deliver my message: that you already have what you're looking for—joy, security, acceptance, peace, and freedom—as your natural state of being. Put simply, you are already that which you seek to be.

So one of the best ways to keep yourself driven and motivated is to write a clear and concise mission statement to remind you of your purpose and remember the 'why' you do what you do.

> Q: Consider when you didn't understand your purpose or when you didn't know why you did what you do. How did it make you feel? What did you do about it?

> Q: Now consider how you would feel if you had a clear and concise mission statement. What would that mission statement be?

YOUR LIFE PURPOSE: INDIVIDUAL, FAMILY, NATIONAL, GLOBAL

When you lack clarity of vision, you will lack clarity of your purpose. When you lack clarity of purpose, you will lack clarity of why you do what you do. When you lack clarity of your 'why', your enthusiasm will drain away. You will lack drive and motivation. Ultimately, you will lack effectiveness.

You know this to be true in your own experience. How many times have you been doing something you weren't interested in doing and said to yourself, "What's the point? It doesn't matter whether I do this or not. Nobody will care."

This lack of enthusiasm is a direct result of your lack of purpose. You see no reason in doing it. The result is inconsequential. You find no meaning in your actions, nor do you put any value in the outcome.

So you give up. You get up and walk away and go and find something that you want to do, something that you value more.

That 'value' you seek is like a treasure you are hunting. Because when you value something, you treasure it. And what you treasure, you keep close to you, you keep it safe and secure.

When it goes missing, you frantically search for it, and this you will keep doing until you find it again and it's once more in your safekeeping.

Having clarity of purpose is like that treasure. When it's close to your heart, you are filled with meaning and enthusiasm for life. When it's lost, you are lost. Your life feels meaningless and you feel disenfranchised, just going through the motions.

When considering your overall Life Purpose, it will help you to focus on four aspects: personal and individual purpose, family and relationship purpose, community and national purpose, and global and humanitarian purpose.

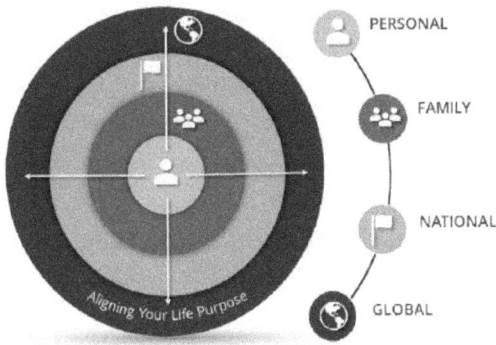

FIGURE 5:   Aligning Your Life Purpose

A good way is to start big and work smaller. For instance, begin by targeting your global purpose, then your community or national purpose, then your family purpose, and then your individual purpose.

In this manner, you will naturally align these four aspects of your overall 'Life Purpose' and you will naturally align with the enthusiasm and passion that drives this purpose.

To use my own Life Purpose as an example, my global or humanitarian purpose is to help humanity become an awakened species. This I do through writing personal development books that are available worldwide, providing online self-help courses, international speaking, and publishing motivational videos and podcasts via my social media channels and my personal website.

My community or national purpose is to connect with people in my local area and in other cities and regional towns that want to improve their relationships, boost their confidence, lift their well-being, increase their effectiveness, and reduce their stress. This I do through my coaching and mentoring programs, public speaking, face-to-face and online workshops, and my books.

My family and relationship purpose is to provide a safe and non-judgemental space in which my immediate and extended family members, friends, colleagues, and associates can have an open discussion about the meaning of life, God, spirituality, love, sexuality, religion, politics, hope, faith, and any other topic important to them without the fear of being labelled, dismissed, or cancelled.

My personal and individual purpose is to awaken to the truth of who I really am and to reflect that truth to the best of my ability through my thoughts, words, actions, and behaviours.

Do I fail? Yes, of course. My thoughts aren't always pure. My emotions sometimes get the better of me. I sometimes say things that I later regret, and my behaviour is sometimes wanting.

But my intention is to always improve, to grow, to learn, to be better today than I was yesterday, and to be better tomorrow than I am today.

> Q: Now consider your global purpose, national purpose, family purpose, and individual purpose. How do these align into your overall 'Life Purpose'?

YOUR PURPOSE: YOUR 1-WORD

Another exercise to get clarity on your purpose, and thus help you to be more effective, is to consider your 7 Life Segments (*see Figure 3: The 7 Life Segments*) and the underlying commonality that unites them.

Of course, *you* are the underlying commonality that unites your 7 Life Segments, but what is the thread that weaves everything you say you are with everything you do? What is the thread that weaves your being with your doing?

In my own life to date, my general experience includes being a son, brother and cousin, a student at school and university. A traveler, a boyfriend, a husband, a mate, a friend, a foe, a father. A co-worker, a bartender, a waiter, a barista. A cricketer, a footballer, a hockey player, a poker player. And more.

In my professional career I've been a medical doctor, a writer, a publisher, a digital marketer, a professional speaker, and a transformational coach.

I searched for a long time to find a word that best described who I am and see myself as being, a transformational messenger, with all my different and varying career paths. It was difficult, but I eventually created my own word—*Life Practitioner*.

> Q: What is your '1-Word' that best describes who you are and what you do? Why did you choose this word? You can create your own word if you need to.

Main Points:

1. Getting clarity on who you are and what you are striving to achieve is vital if you are going to be more effective.
2. The things you do on a day-to-day basis can be divided into 7 Life Segments.
3. Your purpose is your reason for being who you are, doing what you do, and how you do it.
4. You cannot do without being, but you can be without doing.
5. Who you are being is the cause, and what you are doing is the effect.
6. What you do is imbued with the essence of your being—who you are is how you act.
7. Elevate who you are being and you elevate what you do.
8. The RETAINED Model™ describes the main drivers of motivation for people: Remuneration, Education, Trust, Appreciation, Involvement, New Opportunities, Empowerment, Drive & Motivation.
9. When you have clarity of purpose, you are filled with meaning and enthusiasm for life.
10. Align your Life Purpose with your global, national, family, and individual purpose.
11. Your '1-Word' best describes who you are and what you do.

3 THOUGHT, EMOTION & SENSATION

'The only limits you have are the limits you believe.'

Wayne Dyer

IF YOUR EFFECTIVENESS, and therefore your success, is dependent on how you think, it's important to understand how that thinking organ we call the brain works and functions.

To build your effectiveness, you will need to understand the link between your thoughts, emotions, and sensations, and how they can either support or sabotage your attempts to reach your desired state (see *The Process of Transformation*).

Your brain is an essential organ for life and an important conduit of your experience, a neuroelectrical interface that connects your mind's awareness with your body and emotions.

As an interface, your brain facilitates the sharing and exchange of information between your mind, energy, and matter components, expressed as three main types of perception:

1. Psychological—Thoughts (ideas, images, insight, inspiration, memory, foresight, beliefs, creativity).

2. Physiological—Emotions (fear, anxiety, love, pleasure and pain, empathy).

3. Physical—Sensations (the five senses, fight and flight, instincts, reflexes, immunity, movement).

Although on the surface, thoughts, emotions, and sensations appear to be different, they are in fact not distinct from one another. Just as three colours, red, green, and blue, create the spectrum of colours you see on a TV or computer screen, so too your thoughts, emotions, and sensations create the spectrum of experience you see on the screen of your mind.

All three forms are just variations of your perceptual awareness appearing to be dissimilar. But they are not. They are just different vibrational levels of perception communicating information that, when mixed together, are interpreted as an experience in a particular moment in time and space.

For our purposes, though, we will discuss thoughts, emotions, and sensations as individual parts of a 3-in-1 system, like links in a chain, as *Figure 6* illustrates.

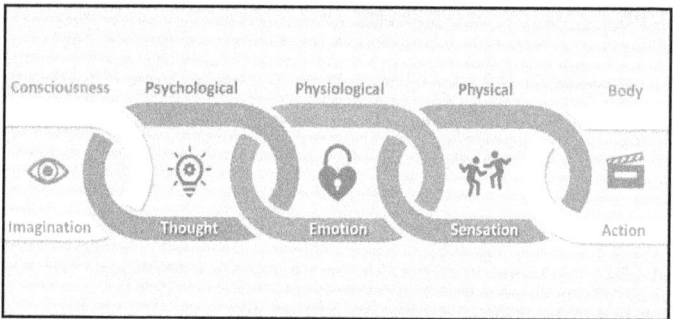

FIGURE 6:   The Chain of Thought,
Emotion & Sensation

Every action first begins as a thought. It is perhaps more accurate to say that every action first begins with your imagination, because you use your conscious imagination to energise and bring to life all your thoughts and ideas. These thoughts and ideas only exist because they are first conceived in your consciousness and born in your imagination.

From imagination, your thoughts and ideas present on the screen of your mind as psychological energy packets, or images. These energetic thought images then trigger a physiological response, which you experience as emotive energy, an emotion.

These emotive energy packets in turn trigger a physical response, often felt bodily as activity or movement, a physical sensation. This physical sensation then triggers an urge or impulse to take an action or encourage a behavioural response.

There is therefore a direct flow of energy transition from your thoughts to your emotions to your actions:

Thought Energy —> Emotive Energy —> Physical Energy

You can do an experiment right now to instantly experience this chain of thought-emotion-sensation:

- -> Think of a time last summer when the mosquitos were out in force.
- -> Recall how you were being bitten by the mosquitos.
- -> Also recall how itchy the bites were on your ankles, arms, and neck.
- -> How do you feel now? Can you feel an itchy sensation? Do you have an urge to scratch?

The emotions and sensations you experience with this exercise are purely created by your own imagination. The annoyance of being bitten, the itch on your neck, the urge to scratch, have simply been triggered by your thoughts about the mosquitos.

The mosquitos are no longer real, but the reactions to your thoughts about them are very real. This has implications for how you think, feel, and react every day.

> *If you don't recognise and take responsibility for the role you play in creating your moment-to-moment life experience, then you condemn yourself to repeating past mistakes and failing to break through your barriers.*

When you perform any action with consideration and thought, you act consciously. You 'ably' respond with 'response-able' action.

If, however, you perform an action without due consideration or thought, you react subconsciously, which is a reflex or a reactive habit.

As you would assume, conscious 'response-able' action is the kind of self-leadership that builds effectiveness, whereas unconscious, habitual reactions generally limit effectiveness.

There is no point in blaming others, God, or circumstances for your current experience. It's actually disempowering and self-defeating.

To use excuses and to blame others is to live your life unconsciously. Which, ultimately, results in poor self-management and the failure to build effectiveness, with the inevitable consequence of failing to live the life you want.

THE INTERPLAY OF THOUGHTS, EMOTIONS & SENSATIONS

There are probably hundreds of times in the past when you wished you could take back what you had said to someone, or you wished you had stopped yourself from doing what you had done.

Or there may be times when you wish you had spoken up instead of remaining silent, or you wish you had taken a different course of action than the one you had.

To better understand the chain of thought-emotion-sensation playing out in your mind thousands of times each day, let's use an imaginary scenario of sending an email that our fictional character, Sally, later regretted.

Sally is a graphic designer who had just received an email from an ungrateful client refusing to pay the invoice for the service she had provided.

The client is unhappy, they write, with the redesign of the logo they had requested. They then proceed to list all their grievances with the quality of Sally's service.

Sally, having been up past midnight working on the project to meet the client's unrealistic deadline, immediately thinks that the client is being unreasonable and unfair.

'How dare they! Don't they know how much work I've put into this project?' she grumbles, unaware that the chain of thought-emotion-sensation has now been set into motion:

    #1: Thought Link—"I am right! They are wrong!"

Almost instantly, Sally's aggrieved thought turns into an aggrieved emotion, anger.

>   #2: Emotion Link—"I'm so angry at him!"

She now begins to feel perspiration beading on her brow, her heart is now racing, and she is even clenching her jaw.

>   #3: Sensation Link—"I feel hot under the collar!"

Sally's psychological, physiological, and physical state has gone from "All is okay this fine morning," to "I'm going to murder someone!" in a fraction of a second.

At this point, Sally is in danger of doing something she might regret later on. Which she does.

Oblivious to the red flags, Sally types a reply to the client's email, letting him know just what she thinks of his miserly attitude and unrealistic expectations, even writing her own list of grievances with him as a client.

The second she hits SEND, however, she is swamped with thoughts of regret, triggering another chain-reaction of thought-emotion-sensation:

>   #1: Thought Link—"I shouldn't have done that!"
>   #2: Emotion Link—"I'm going to pay for this!"
>   #3: Sensation Link—"I feel sick in the stomach!"

Sally's fluctuating thoughts, emotions, and feelings have all occurred before her morning cup of coffee has even cooled. The rest of the day is still yet to be played out.

Unbeknown to her, Sally has suffered from her own lack of awareness of what's going on inside, to her own detriment.

What Sally needs, and what will help her in the future when another Mr. Grumpy pays her a visit, which he surely will, is to fully understand the chain of thought-emotion-sensation.

Had she been aware of the links between her thoughts and actions, she would have better self-managed her response and built greater effectiveness for herself and for her client.

> Q: What are some instances where you said or did something, or didn't say or do something, that you later regretted? Try to recall what you were thinking, what emotions you had, and what you were physically feeling at that time.

FILTERS OF AWARENESS

The main problem that Sally faces is her lack of awareness. Her lack of awareness is the main reason she is oblivious to the links between her thoughts and her actions, and why she fails to act response-ably and build her effectiveness.

Sally's lack of awareness is what gets her into trouble with her client. The solution, therefore, to prevent Sally repeating her mistakes and getting into more trouble, is for Sally to become more mindful of how her thoughts, emotions, and behaviours are interlinked.

Sally is behaving like a flea in a flea circus, unaware of her true potential. She therefore needs to become more mindful of the causative link between her thoughts and her subsequent behaviours.

Until she does, she will keep repeating the same mistakes over and over again, much to the detriment of her business and her personal life.

The first step is for Sally to understand what's blocking her awareness of the chain of thought, emotion, and sensation. Once she understands what's blocking her, she will be able to unblock her awareness and begin to better manage her responses and build her effectiveness.

She will be able to transcend her self-imposed limitations and escape the flea circus.

Belief, Emotion, Instinct

Previously, we discussed how your mindset orientation, or perspective, determines your point of view and how you see yourself interacting with the world around you.

Part of your perspective is developed by your beliefs, emotions, and natural instincts, which are wired into the neurocircuitry of your brain.[5]

This is because you see the world through three main filters of awareness: what you *believe* to be true about yourself and the world; your background *emotional* state of being; and your natural *instincts* for safety and survival. Nothing you see or experience goes unfiltered.

---

[5] The Triune Theory of the human brain, Paul MacLean

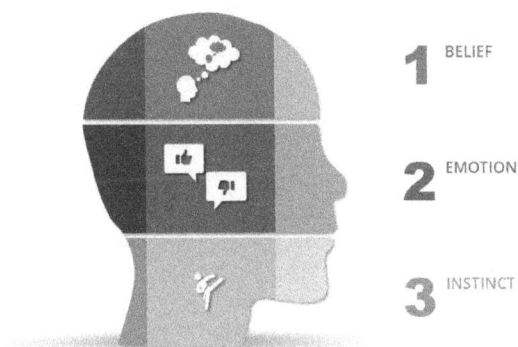

FIGURE 7:   Filters of Awareness

For instance, if you believe for whatever reason that you don't deserve success or that you aren't good enough, then your mind will filter everything it receives through that belief system and present to your conscious awareness a picture that reinforces and supports that belief about yourself—powerlessness, failure, rejection, worthlessness, futility, submission.

If your background or underlying emotional state of being is anger, then your mind will filter everything it receives through that emotional state and present to your conscious awareness a picture that reinforces and supports that angry state of being—injustice, victimisation, frustration, hatred, sexism, aggression, isolation, violence.

If your natural instincts for safety and survival are not held in check, your mind will filter everything it receives through that heightened sense of threat and present to your conscious awareness a picture that reinforces and supports that fear—illness anxiety, refusal to take risks, conspiracy, fear of strangers, lack of trust, abandonment.

Your beliefs, emotions, and natural instincts are therefore a palette with which your mind paints the picture of who you say you are or want to see.

> *Your mind paints a picture of what you accept or agree about yourself.*

At the back of a cinema before digital projectors superceded analogue projectors, a movie reel was passed over a projector lens at 24 frames per second. A beam of light from the projector passing through the moving frames of the reel cast the movie onto the silver screen for the audience to watch.

The beam of light didn't care what was on the film. Whatever was on the movie reel was what was projected onto the screen.

The same is true for the 'movie reel' you play inside your mind.

> *What you think, how you feel, how you react, is projected onto the 'silver screen' inside your mind and that's what you see.*

In other words, your mind tells you what you are seeing or going to see. This is the power of 'what is behind your eyes'.

However, like the power of electricity, which can either kill or provide life-giving energy, your mind must be properly directed before it becomes a source of power. It must be trained before it can be used to your advantage.

Be mindful, then, that your mind can either work for you, or it can work against you—your mind can either help you to overcome your limitations, or, like a flea in a flea circus, it can keep you contained within your own self-imposed limits.

Especially if any of these mental habits relate to you:

- Self-limiting beliefs about yourself.
- Underlying biases and hidden prejudices.
- Thinking you know everything there is to know.
- Black and white thinking.
- Constant fear of failure.
- Jumping to conclusions, persistent assumptions, or unrealistic expectations.
- Cynicism and constant doubt.
- Small-mindedness and missing the big picture.

Remember, you are the master of your thoughts, emotions, and instincts. Taking control of these aspects of your mind is therefore essential if you wish to break through your barriers and transcend your limits.

That's where your real power lies—the power to change the movie reel of your life.

Main Points:

1. To build your effectiveness, you will need to understand the link between your thoughts, emotions, and sensations.

2. Every action first begins with your imagination.

3. There is a direct flow of energy transition from your thoughts to your emotions to your actions.

4. Conscious 'response-able' action is the kind of self-leadership that builds effectiveness.

5. Your thoughts, emotions, and sensations create the spectrum of experience you see on the screen of your mind.

6. You see the world through three main filters of awareness: what you *believe*; your *emotional* state; and your natural *instincts*.

7. Your mind paints a picture of what you accept or agree about yourself.

8. You are the master of your thoughts, emotions, and instincts—you have the power to change the movie reel of your life.

4 THE 5 BLOCKS TO BUILDING EFFECTIVENESS

'As my mind can conceive of more good, the barriers and the blocks dissolve.'

Louise Hay

THE SAME FILTERS of awareness that operate within your brain—your beliefs, your emotions, your natural instincts—can also become so clogged that they become not just filters but blockages of awareness.

Not only can these filters manipulate and project what you see about yourself and the world around you, they can also block you from correctly perceiving the truth about yourself and the outside world.

When untrained, your own mind can be a barrier to your efforts to better self-manage and build effectiveness. It can habitually block your way and stop you from getting ahead.

Our fictional character, Sally, for instance, is unaware of how her thoughts, emotions, and sensations affect her behaviour. She is blocked from seeing the cause (thoughts, emotions, sensations) of her effect (behaviours, actions, impulses).

The good news is, Sally can unblock her awareness, and so can you. Which means you can start to reap the benefits of greater effectiveness and escape the flea circus almost immediately.

All that's required to remove your blocks is: 1) know and accept that you have blocks; 2) desire and intend to remove your blocks; 3) understand what blocks exist; and 4) focus the light of attention onto your blocks (discussed next chapter).

Assuming that you now know and accept that you have blocks of awareness and that you also wish to remove them, we now need to understand what blocks exist. As a general rule, there are 5 BLOCKs to our awareness that we should be mindful of:

-> **B**: Blinded by the Light—distractions.

-> **L**: Likes and Dislikes—personal bias.

-> **O**: Overthinking and Overwhelm—mental clutter.

-> **C**: Cynicism and Despair—negative worldview.

-> **K**: Killjoy Attitude—mental anaemia.

These 5 BLOCKs arise from the three parts of our triune brain:[6] reptilian, paleomammalian, and neomammalian.

Located at the rear of the skull where it meets the spinal cord, the reptilian hindbrain, the oldest and least evolved part of our brain, is responsible for our primitive reactions and our survival instinct.

When our safety is threatened, it is our reptilian brain that kicks into action with fight, flight or freeze.

---

[6] Please note: although some neuroscientists consider the Triune Brain Theory outdated, it is still an interesting model of how the different parts of our brain interact with each other. If you sliced open a human brain at autopsy, you will not find such neatly delineated sections of the brain. As such, it is best considered a theoretical model of how the brain works and functions, not a model of its physical anatomy.

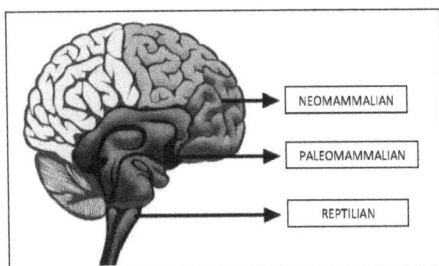

FIGURE 8:   The Triune Brain

The paleomammalian midbrain ('paleo' means old), located in the outer central part of the brain, is also known as the limbic system. It is a more evolved area of the brain than the reptilian brain, and it is responsible for emotional processing, long-term memory, dreams, and smelling.

For our discussion, we will consider the paleomammalian brain that area in control of our pleasure and pain responses.

The neomammalian forebrain ('neo' means new), located in the outer frontal part of the brain, is the most evolved area of the human brain. It is responsible for our superior intelligence and is perhaps that part of the brain which separates humans from the rest of the animal kingdom.

For our discussion, we will consider the neomammalian brain that area in control of our higher reasoning, analysis, planning, foresight, beliefs, and self-awareness.

Let's now discuss the 5 BLOCKs of awareness in relation to these three areas of our brain so that we can transcend our self-imposed limits and escape the flea circus.

B: Blinded by the Light

The first block to be aware of is how easily you are blinded by the lights. This is not the paralysis of a deer at headlights approaching along the highway, rather how easily you are dazzled and distracted by the five senses of sight, sound, touch, taste, and smell.

When we find it difficult to stay focused and to concentrate for long periods of time, our attention can be seduced by 'bright shiny objects'.

"Oh, look at this!" "Oh, look at that!" "Oh, look over here!"

Bright, sparkly things attract our attention, and sensory distraction is one of the main causes of procrastination. It is also one of the major blocks to building effectiveness because it removes your focus from important, substantive matters and redirects it to less important, fleeting matters with little or no substance.

Our attention is constantly being distracted, which, generally speaking, probably has something to do with the rapid rise of technology over the past two decades or so. You only need to walk into a restaurant or hop on a train to see how many people are dazzled by their mobile phones.

Because of modern technology, we are now inundated with information and overloaded with sensory stimuli. We therefore have to be more selective in what we focus on, even if we think that not concentrating on the task at hand isn't a problem.

But consider the direct costs of this. How much effectiveness have you failed to capitalise on because you are too easily distracted or too easily disengaged? How much effectiveness have you actually lost or wasted because you couldn't concentrate long enough on what needed to be done?

The issue of sensory distraction, though, is biological, not technical, because its roots lie in the paleomammalian midbrain's concepts of pleasure and pain.

In essence, your midbrain wants you to run towards that which gives you pleasure, and it wants you to run away from that which causes you pain. As such, sensory distraction falls into two categories: arousal and avoidance.

Arousal distraction is when you deliberately distract yourself from what you are doing, or should be doing, by seeking out pleasurable or effortless activities over tasks you find tiresome or boring. You are tempted to seek a quick 'pleasure fix'.

For instance, instead of doing the ironing, you watch TV or play computer games. Instead of writing that business proposal or submitting your tax return, you check your social media feed or search the internet for cheap flights for your next holiday.

> Q: What are some instances where you deliberately distracted yourself from doing what you should do at home and at work?

Avoidance distraction is when you deliberately do other tasks than the one that you know you should be doing. What you are really doing is avoiding the pain of emotional, intellectual, or physical hard work.

For instance, instead of having that difficult conversation with your teenage daughter, you mow the lawns or do the grocery shopping. Instead of ringing that client and following up on their inquiry, you check your emails or have a chat with a fellow co-worker about this week's football game.

> Q: What are some instances where you deliberately
>   avoided doing what you should do at home and
>   at work?

Sensory distraction can become a habit if you are not aware of your thoughts, emotions, and behaviours. There is nothing wrong in seeking pleasure at appropriate moments. The problem is when we continually seek pleasure all day, every day, non-stop.

Why? Because we become addicted to the thing that gives us pleasure—food, drugs, cigarettes, sex, our career, power, gaming, money, travel, fitness, entertainment, gambling. The list is endless. Almost anything that gives us pleasure can become an addiction if we feel we need it to feel good about ourself.

So when our sensory distraction is a habit, it becomes psychologically addictive, an obsession, which is a major internal block. If you do nothing about it, you will eventually suffer the psychological equivalent of constipation, which is mental stuckness.

You will then need more and more sensory distraction to satisfy your longing for pleasure, or satisfy your need to avoid pain and discomfort, to get unstuck. Like a chain-smoker, you will spend every waking moment trying to satisfy those cravings.

Anyone with an obsessive or addictive 'sensory' habit will find it difficult to build effectiveness because all their energy and mental focus is invested in satisfying their senses. Their life becomes severely limited to the pursuit of pleasure and avoidance of pain, just another flea in the flea circus.

So what's the problem with feeling good about ourself? Nothing, except if you think you need something other than yourself to feel good about yourself. Then you become disempowered, all of your own doing.

You disempower yourself by giving your power away to that thing or person you think you need to feel good. You disempower yourself when you think you can't be happy, or peaceful, or safe, or acceptable without some other person or some other thing.

This is why addiction to bright shiny objects is disempowering, why continually being blinded by the light and constantly being distracted keeps you stuck in your own limitations and prevents you from escaping the flea circus:

Because it blinds you to your own inner power.

The way out of sensory addiction is a 4-step process, which we will discuss in the next chapter, *Let it Rain*.

> Q: Consider when you have been easily distracted and continually sought out that person or thing that gave you pleasure. What was the effect to your personal or professional life? Did you feel empowered or disempowered by this behaviour? What did you do about it?

L: Likes and Dislikes

The next block to be aware of is your own likes and dislikes. Personal preferences and aversions are normal, and they generally won't interfere with your attempts to build effectiveness unless they become narrow and discriminatory.

The consequence of having narrow and stubborn likes and dislikes, however, is to close the mind and shut yourself off to other opportunities that present to you each and every moment.

Yet your mind, as they say, is like a parachute—it works best when open.

For instance, the difference between a professional and a hobbyist is that the professional will always work no matter the situation or what mood she is in, whereas the hobbyist will only work when the situation is right and when the mood suits him. This is the difference between *mind* motivation and *mood* motivation.

Having a hobby is great, but not when it's your profession. You can't bring a hobby mindset to your work and expect to have a successful career.

Working only when you feel like it, or when you are in the right mood, doesn't make you a professional, nor is it good self-management. Working only when your workspace is perfect and everything is in order, or only at a time of your choosing, isn't a recipe for success, it's a recipe for stagnation.

The main difference between a professional mindset and a

hobbyist attitude is the ability to cope and get on with it when things are 'not right' or the way you want them to be. It's the ability to put aside your personal preferences and expectations and move forward despite how you're feeling.

But here's the key:

> *People with good self-management habits know that even if they aren't in the 'right mood' to do the work they need to do, the act of working will put them in the mood they want.*

For example, the best time to go to the gym and workout is when you are putting it off and don't feel like it. The hardest part is walking through the entrance into the gym. Once you're there and exercising, you start to feel better for it.

But if you wait to take action only when the outside world is perfect and right, according to your evaluation, or you wait until you're in the right mood, you will limit yourself only to what you like and dislike, which is very narrow.

The effect is akin to wearing a pair of Polaroid sunglasses that filters the entire world into that which you like and that which you don't like, that which you accept and that which you reject.

Consequently, your world will become very polarised. "I like her, I don't like him." "I like red, I don't like blue." "I like dogs, I don't like cats."

When this happens, like our fictional character, Sally, the

world has to conform to your preferences and expectations in order for you to feel comfortable and at peace with yourself.

Like Sally, if the world doesn't conform to your preferences or expectations, you will try to force it to conform. You will become controlling and manipulative. You will micro-manage others. You will become needy and dependent.

But how can you control everything and everyone?

You can't. Neither can Sally. Which is a problem for both of you. Like Sally, you'll get frustrated when things don't happen the way you planned them to. You'll get angry when others don't conform to your ideas of correct behaviour. Or worse, when they vote for a different political party than the one you voted for. Or they believe in a different god.

So you withdraw and only allow yourself to be surrounded by like-minded people who believe the same as you and won't challenge those beliefs you hold so dear to your heart.

You start to live in a silo. Just as Sally would do, you give exclusive and preferential treatment to those who support your likes and dislikes. You create an 'Us vs Them' mentality, further polarising your world, which inevitably leads to increasing competitiveness and hostility to those you deem 'outside' your immediate clan.

In order to maintain order and calm, you naturally tighten your control over the world you have created. You start to feel ill-will to those you have excluded because they have now become an existential threat to your self-identity.

They must not be allowed to rock the boat under any circumstances. Even the slightest threat to your status quo invokes jealousy, hatred, anger, and other negative emotions. Physical violence becomes an extremely valid option.

And all because you need to defend your likes and dislikes and have your world to be in a certain way.

So here's the issue. The problem, again, lies in your triune brain. Your likes give you pleasure, and your dislikes cause you pain. Like the first BLOCK of sensory distraction, this is your pleasure and pain centre—your paleomammalian midbrain—influencing your thoughts and feelings and behaviours.

When you like something or someone, you feel good. When you don't like something or someone, you don't feel good. Feeling good is pleasurable. Not feeling good is not pleasurable.

We like feeling good, so we keep liking that thing or person that makes us feel good in a positively reinforcing cycle of thought, emotion, and behaviour—we keep seeking it out.

We also dislike feeling bad. So we keep disliking that thing or person that makes us feel bad in a positively reinforcing cycle of thought, emotion, and behaviour—we keep avoiding it.

In other words, we run to whatever or whoever makes us feel good, and we flee whatever or whoever makes us feel bad.

But as Shakespeare wrote in *Hamlet*,

> *There is nothing either good or bad, but thinking makes it so.*

These words are uttered by Hamlet in Act II, Scene 2, as he grapples with his confinement within Denmark's political web and the oppressive weight of his own mind. The knowledge of his father's murder, executed by King Claudius, gnaws at his very soul, a truth he cannot escape.

But, as Shakespeare was trying to bring to our attention, there is no inherent good or bad in nature; it is our thoughts that create the duality of good and bad, and it is our thoughts that breathe life into such judgements.

In simpler terms, this quote invites us to consider how our thoughts and beliefs shape our perception of the world. It suggests that what we label as 'good' or 'bad' is not an objective reality but rather a product of our individual perspectives.

Which means we are in control of what we deem as either good or bad. We are in control of what we like and dislike.

Problems arise when we forget this, or rather, when we are blocked from being aware of this. When we relinquish control of the only thing that we can control—our inner thoughts and beliefs.

Patterns of behaviour become established, often for a lifetime, and often beyond our awareness of how we are behaving, when we unconsciously submit to the whims of our likes and dislikes.

This is personal bias, and even hidden prejudice. Like Sally, we lean a certain way toward people or situations (bias) and we prejudge certain events or people (prejudice).

When taken to its extreme, the risk of bias and prejudice is that relationships can be destroyed. Friendships can be ruined. Careers can be lost. Money can be squandered. Lives can be wasted.

All because we habitually cling to the notion of 'what I like is good, and what I dislike is bad'. All because we identify with our personal biases and hidden prejudices.

This is why rigid adherence to what you like and what you dislike can keep you stuck in your own limitations and prevent you from escaping the flea circus:

> *Because it smothers your ability to control your inner world.*

We will discuss the ways out of this block in the next chapter.

> Q: Consider when you have been easily manipulated
> by your own likes or dislikes. What was the effect
> to your personal or professional life? Did you feel
> in control of this behaviour or situation? What
> did you do about it?

O: Overthinking and Overwhelm

One of the defining characteristics of being human is our wonderful ability to think: to reason, to plan, to analyse, to imagine.

However, overthinking can trip us over if we're not careful, and it can be another stumbling block to building effectiveness.

Overthinking is not an instinctive reaction to a perceived threat, rather it is an over-stimulation or excitability of the brain's higher reasoning centres.

This block of awareness is therefore the block of mental clutter. When so much 'stuff' fills our head, it can block our higher reasoning centres from functioning and trap our thinking in an endless loop. This is a problem of our neomammalian forebrain.

When our thinking is trapped, our vision is limited. We can only see what's in front of us. We can't see the bigger picture. We can't see the path out of the woods.

Overthinking takes root in moments of uncertainty, doubt, and vulnerability, when the mind clings to 'what-ifs' and 'what-may-bes'.

It often arises from the desire to make the right choices, to foresee every outcome and eventuality, to control the uncertainties and complexities of life.

Overthinking feels like the relentless churning of the mind's gears. This ceaseless mental activity often occurs in the quiet hours of the night, when the mind is left to its own devices, causing endless worry and anxiety. Worse, preventing the body from getting much needed rest and sleep.

But overthinking isn't confined to nighttime. It can occur any time of the day, especially during times of transition and change, when the path forward is shrouded in mist.

A valid piece of advice from Albert Einstein is to try and

simplify things as much as possible, but not to make it simple. According to Einstein, there is beauty and clarity in simplification.

Those who are habitual overthinkers, however, do not follow this advice. It's as if the more complexity there is, the better it is. Simplification is anathema to an overthinking mind.

Common things to look out for if you suspect yourself of overthinking, include:

- Reading into things that aren't there.
- Overcomplicating matters.
- Making mountains out of molehills.
- Unable to let go of suffocating thoughts.
- Poor attention span and difficulty focusing.
- Obsessive or vengeful thoughts.
- Going around in circles, mental exhaustion.

The biggest issue or problem with overthinking is that it causes a restless and unsettled mind. Your mind can't settle in the present moment because it is caught in worries of the future, or regrets and judgement of the past.

This restlessness and unsettledness has been given a name, 'monkey mind', because the mind is like a monkey jumping from branch to branch, unable to sit still or stay present for any period of time.

The consequence of the overthinking 'monkey mind' is that it has no time to focus. It too easily succumbs to distraction;

and because it is in a perpetual state of unfocused attention, it becomes extremely hard to see clearly and engage in the process of quality decision-making.

This is why persistent overthinking can keep you stuck in your own limitations and prevent you from escaping the flea circus:

Because it overwhelms your capacity to see clearly.

Q: What are some instances where you have been victim to your own overthinking? How did your 'monkey mind' affect your ability to make quality decisions and build effectiveness?

One big problem with overthinking is that it can spiral into overwhelm. Like a computer with too many tabs open, or a mobile phone with too many apps open, the processing capability of the overthinking mind can slow, freeze, or even shutdown completely. Then you need to reboot.

> *Overwhelm is the sense of being completely overcome by intense and uncomfortable thoughts, emotions, and sensations that seem too demanding to manage and overcome.*

When in a state of overwhelm, thought processing can be irrational, emotions can be extreme, and behaviour can be dysfunctional.

Although overwhelm can be positive (for example, bliss, ecstasy), it is most often a negative experience.

There are many things that cause overwhelm, including:

1. Relationship issues.
2. Physical or mental ill health.
3. Work demands.
4. Poor diet/nutrition (including alcohol, cigarettes).
5. Financial hardship/distress.
6. Significant life changes (for example, retirement).
7. Time pressure/deadlines.
8. Death/Loss of a loved one.
9. Personal traumas.
10. Insomnia/Lack of sleep (including new parenting).

Although the causes are many and varied, overwhelm tends to be expressed in three main ways:

1. Mental.
2. Emotional/Physiological.
3. Physical.

As we discussed in *Chapter 3: Thought, Emotion & Sensation*, these three states are interwoven and interpenetrating. When one state is affected, so are the others. Overwhelm therefore involves all three parts of the triune brain, not just the forebrain.

Mentally, overwhelm can manifest as irritability, excessive worry, doubt, helplessness, poor memory, loss of libido.

Emotionally, a person can be overwhelmed by anger, fear, anxiety, hatred, jealousy, guilt, or shame.

Physiologically, the response to overwhelm is the same as any perceived threat. Adrenaline and the steroid hormone, cortisol, also known as the 'stress hormone', flood the body in readiness for the fight and flight response.

Physically, cortisol keeps the body in a continued, heightened sense of alertness, which is a normal response to a perceived threat to your safety or survival.

However, most 'threats' or incidents in your day-to-day world aren't high risk to your safety or survival, but your brain still reacts to each incident in much the same way, by instructing your body to produce copious amounts of stress hormones. This can happen hundreds of times a day.

More so, the brain cannot distinguish between what is real and what is imaginary. It will react the same way to an imaginary threat as it will to a real threat, flooding your body with stress hormones.

Your body goes where your mind goes. So your thoughts, worries, fears, anxieties, and even memories can trigger the fight and flight response just as rapidly and as easily as if you saw a snake slither across your path.

The problem is that your worries and fears can cause you to live in a perpetual state of stress and overwhelm. In this state, a person can become emotionally labile, lash out verbally or physically, or even have a panic attack.

Author's note:

If you have signs or symptoms of overwhelm you are advised to seek medical help to investigate any underlying health problem that may exist.

So let's consider some practical situations where chronic overwhelm can limit your ability to build effectiveness.

As we have discussed, your natural instinct for self-preservation is a trigger for the 'fight and flight' response. But when it becomes overwhelming, it can also cause you to 'freeze', like a deer caught in the headlights of an oncoming vehicle. During your working day, this 'freezing' or paralysis is a significant cause of procrastination and ineffectiveness.

For example, when you feel overwhelmed by a task at work, your reptilian hindbrain goes into 'shutdown', which causes you to put off doing the task at hand and you procrastinate.

There are many reasons to feel stressed at work, such as:

- Tight deadlines.
- Multi-tasking and excessive amounts of work.
- Job insecurity.
- Unsafe work environment.
- High expectations (from clients, staff, bosses, self).
- High skill level requirements.
- High levels of responsibility.
- High costs of failure (death, financial loss, legal).

In such circumstances, you can feel overwhelmed and even powerless to do what you need to do. You might believe that you don't have the necessary skills to perform the task at hand or finish in the allotted time. You might also feel unsupported and isolated, left to fend for yourself.

This sense of overwhelm and isolation can just as easily happen at home as it can at work. But in whatever situation it arises, the causes of overwhelm, especially persistent and continuous, need to be addressed in order to manage your mental, emotional, and physical well-being.

Only then will you be in a position of strength to focus on building your effectiveness.

We will discuss the ways out of this block in the next chapter.

> Q: What are some instances where you have felt inundated and unable to cope? How did this effect your thoughts, emotions, and behaviour? What or who triggers this overwhelm to recur?

C: Cynicism & Doubt

The next block to be aware of is cynicism and doubt.

Cynicism, in fact, is more than just a stumbling block, it is a major roadblock. Of all the 5 BLOCKs to building effectiveness, cynicism is perhaps the most entrenched and thus most difficult to overcome.

The problem with cynicism is that it suffocates and strangles your positive thoughts and intentions before they can take root and grow, much like noxious weeds suffocating and strangling any other sapling trying to grow in the same soil.

Cynicism is to the intellect what despair is to the emotions. It is the intellectual equivalent of the feeling of hopelessness, and there is more than just a touch of sad pessimism to everything the cynic thinks, says, and does.

The cynic may feel clever and wise, even intellectually superior, but his cynicism is actually a defence mechanism to protect himself from the pain of disappointment.

Cynicism isn't realism, yet the cynic will always claim to be 'a realist', to see things as they truly are. But that's just a distortion of the truth, a distortion to try and fit 'reality' into his worldview that things will only get worse before they get worse.

The true reality of the cynical mindset is a rejection of the world as it is. The motto of the cynic is to shoot first and ask questions later. Shoot it down before it can hurt you. Quickly snuff the life out of it before it has a chance to breathe.

The root cause of cynicism is the belief that things won't work out the way you want them to. This is usually because past experience and disappointments have drummed into you the futility of hoping your efforts will create the outcome you truly want.

Or because you've been taught to believe things will never change for the better by your parents, friends, or society.

Cynicism limits you. It closes you off and isolates you from the rest of the world. The out-of-hand rejection of things to protect yourself from hurt or disappointment is ultimately self-defeating because all it does is keep you in a perpetual state of stagnation.

But to grow and move forward you must cast off the yoke of cynicism and embrace your vulnerability, to allow things to go wrong, to let yourself fail, to take risks.

Because only through embracing the possibility of being hurt and experiencing disappointment can you embrace the possibility of what you are truly capable of being.

> Q: What are some instances where you have been overly cynical? What were you trying to protect about yourself? How did cynicism affect your ability to build effectiveness?

Doubt, especially sceptical doubt, is a diluted form of cynicism. Not every sceptic is cynical, but every cynic is sceptical.

In science, scepticism is revered. Every new idea or theory is met with a healthy dose of scepticism before it is accepted as a scientific fact. A good scientist just doesn't accept a new idea without putting it through the rigours of rejection and derision.

Even Einstein's theories on relativity were initially met with scorn and disbelief when they were first published. But that's how the science world progresses. Scientific advancement only occurs along the slow, windy road of doubt. New norms are only accepted once old norms have been shown to be redundant, which can take generations.

But you don't have generations. You only have this one life, and your time is always ticking down. Scientific scepticism and doubt might work in the world of science, but on an individual level too much scepticism and doubt can actually slow you down and be detrimental.

The problem is that scepticism and doubt clog your decision-making apparatus, grinding it to a halt, which leads to indecisiveness.

The type of doubts that can clog your mental machinery are thoughts that cause you to question who you are, what you're doing, why you're doing it, even how, where, and when you're doing it.

You know you are victim to your own scepticism and doubt and are guilty of putting a spanner in your own works when you get lost in thoughts such as:

- Am I doing the right thing?
- What will they think of me?
- What if I'm not ready?
- When will be the right time to do it?
- How can I be certain that it will work?

When the mind gets clogged by scepticism and doubt, you cannot align and synchronise your intentions with your actions. Like a train engine decoupling from its carriages, a separation or disengagement with your goals and aspirations occurs. When this happens, your doubts have all but caused you to come to a complete stop in your tracks.

To get moving forward again, you will need to clear the scepticism and doubt from your mind and allow clarity of thought to recouple with your goals and aspirations.

This is why persistent cynicism and doubt can keep you stuck in your own limitations and prevent you from escaping the flea circus:

Because it decouples you from your true potential.

We will discuss the ways out of this block in the next chapter.

> Q: What are some instances where you have been
> lost in self-doubt? How did your doubts affect
> your ability to build effectiveness?

K: Killjoy Attitude

The final block to be aware of is your killjoy attitude. This literally means to kill the joy in every moment.

With this attitude, it's hard to accept that anyone else can be happy, which is why you kill the joy around you. When happiness arises in yourself, or comes to you from others, you stamp it out. You make sure it doesn't last very long, if at all.

Like Sally, you likely suffer from a killjoy attitude when you think and behave like Scrooge or the Christmas Grinch:

- You get irritated by children's laughter.
- You make snide remarks about others.
- You are dismissive of other's ideas or intentions.
- It's your way or the highway.
- It grates you when others are successful.
- You can't suffer fools.

Mental dullness and feelings of physical heaviness are the two main symptoms of a chronic killjoy attitude.

Mental dullness is a kind of torpor, a waking sleepiness, where you might be up and out of bed but you're not really awake or alert to what's happening around you. The lights are on but nobody's home.

This is not a lack of sleep or exhaustion, rather a state of mental anaemia that manifests as a dampened or sluggish alertness, which is partially borne by the stubborn refusal to allow yourself any modicum of enthusiasm.

This is a problem of belief, of how you see yourself interact with the world around you, and is therefore a blockage of your neomammalian forebrain.

You just won't let yourself get excited about anything. Not that you can't get excited, which is one of the clinical symptoms of major depression, it's just that you won't allow yourself to.

That's the difference between clinical depression and a killjoy attitude—choice. A person with depression doesn't choose to be depressed, but someone with a killjoy attitude does choose to be a killjoy.

So when you feel that emerging thrill of excitement coming to the surface, you immediately deprive it of oxygen. You smother it time and time again until there's no sign of life.

After years of suffocating your enthusiasm, it barely registers in your awareness anymore. You've become so adept you kill it off subconsciously. It's become a habit.

With a killjoy habit, not only do you have a problem of mental sluggishness, but you also have symptoms of physical sluggishness. This you begin to feel as a lack of energy, a muscular or bodily heaviness that weighs you down and eventually manifests as slothfulness or laziness.

In the end, all you do is dig a metaphorical pit into which you jump and imprison yourself. In this hole, it's difficult to make any mental or physical effort. You can't be bothered to even lift a finger.

When in this state, your ability to build effectiveness is all but non-existent. This is why a persistent killjoy attitude can keep you stuck in your own limitations and prevent you from escaping the flea circus:

> *Because it suffocates the joyous expression of life, who you really are.*

We will discuss the ways out of this block in the next chapter.

> Q: What are some instances where you have been a killjoy? How did this attitude affect your ability to build effectiveness?

MAIN POINTS:

1. When untrained, your own mind can be a barrier to your efforts to better self-manage and build effectiveness.

2. As a general rule, there are 5 BLOCKs to our awareness that we should be mindful of.

3. These 5 BLOCKs arise from the three parts of our triune brain: reptilian, paleomammalian, and neomammalian.

4. Addiction to 'bright shiny objects' is disempowering because it blinds you to your own inner power.

5. Rigid adherence to what you like and what you dislike smothers your ability to control your inner world.

6. Persistent overthinking overwhelms your capacity to see clearly.

7. Persistent cynicism decouples you from your true potential.

8. A persistent killjoy attitude suffocates the joyous expression of life, who you really are.

5 LET IT RAIN

'The world can only change from within.'

Eckhart Tolle

Now we know the 5 BLOCKS to building effectiveness, what can we do about them? How can we turn our blocks into building blocks?

Prevention, of course, is better than the cure. So, if you can, you need to structure and align your mindset in such a way to prevent those blocks from arising.

This requires a good dose of mental fortitude and constant mindfulness, which is not easy. So, if your efforts are not successful in preventing these blocks from arising, you need to implement some kind of cure, which will involve employing certain techniques in order to extract or remove your blocks.

Each of these 5 BLOCKs is preventing you from building effectiveness and is neutralising your efforts to live a more complete and fulfilling life. In order to sidestep these blocks, all you need to remember, as the Buddhists say, is to 'Let it RAIN'.

This is a 4-step method to help you remove your blocks and give yourself the best opportunity to build effectiveness.

To 'Let it RAIN', all you need to do is:

-> **R:** Recognise the symptoms.

-> **A:** Accept what is.

-> **I:** Identify the cause.

-> **N:** Navigate your way out.

R: Recognise the Symptoms

The problem most people encounter is that they don't recognise the symptoms of the 5 BLOCKs for what they are and what they signify. Unfortunately, most people don't know what they don't know.

Even if the symptoms of being blocked are noticed, it's easy to dismiss these symptoms as irrelevant and nothing to worry about. Or to associate these symptoms with something else, usually something minor or insignificant.

But as we know, symptoms are warning signs of something going on underneath your awareness. If left unchecked, symptoms of an underlying problem will only become more intense and more frequent, until, more often than not, it's too late to do anything about the underlying cause or issue.

Recognising the symptoms of the 5 BLOCKs for what they are—markers of the underlying state of your mind—is the vital first step in eliminating these blocks.

You can only implement a solution to a problem that you know exists. Awareness, then, is the key. Awareness of what state of mind you are in.

BLOCK	SYMPTOMS
B: Blinded by the Lights	-Poor attention span. -Easily distracted. -Avoidance behaviour. -Sensory addiction.
L: Likes & Dislikes	-Closed-mindedness. -Controlling behaviour. -Motivated by mood states. -Ill-will toward others/things.
O: Overthinking & Overwhelm	-Restless or unsettled mind. -Intense and uncomfortable thoughts, emotions, sensations. -Feelings of being unable to cope. -Continual over-reaction.
C: Cynicism & Doubt	-Intellectual superiority. -Futility, hopelessness, despair. -Chronic indecisiveness.
K: Killjoy Attitude	-Refusal to feel enthusiastic. -Mental sluggishness. -Physical heaviness.

TABLE 2:   The 5 BLOCKs & Associated Symptoms

You may recognise symptoms in yourself of one or more of these 5 BLOCKs, maybe even all of them. Which is actually great news, because now you can take steps to do something about them.

A: Accept What Is

Before you can implement a solution to your blocks and navigate your way around them, you first need to accept that you have a problem.

Denying that you have a block, or rejecting any idea or notion that it exists, will only cement that block in place and make it harder for you to remove.

In her famous book, *On Death and Dying*,[7] psychiatrist Dr. Elisabeth Kübler-Ross first outlined her theory of the 5 Stages of Grief—Denial, Anger, Bargaining, Depression, Acceptance.

Her underlying philosophy was that everyone would best be served by gracefully accepting that death and dying is an integral and necessary part of life.

In her research, Kübler-Ross recognised that most, if not all, terminally ill patients who went through the grieving process of their own death struggled to come to terms with their own mortality.

Those that did manage to arrive at a final acceptance of their impending death, despite their circumstances, died with great peace and little suffering.

But they had to journey to this place of acceptance; they didn't just arrive there. Although some journeyed quicker than others, all experienced in various degrees the states of denial, anger, bargaining, and depression before they arrived at a place of complete acceptance.

---

[7] Elisabeth Kübler-Ross, *On Death and Dying*, Macmillan, 1969

As with any grief, Kübler-Ross recognised that a person is most likely to at first deny that they are terminally ill and dying. There is fear of loss, fear of the unknown, fear of the end.

"No, not me," is the common reaction. "Why me? Why now? I'm not ready. This can't be true."

Often upon hearing the diagnosis of a terminal disease, the patient would demand a second opinion, or demand more investigations in the hope the original diagnosis was wrong.

Anger is also a common reaction. Anger at the illness. Anger at themselves, at others, at God. Anger with the situation. Anger at their helplessness and lack of control.

Many patients die in this state of anger, never reaching full acceptance of their impending death. Others, however, try to bargain or buy their way out of death.

They bargain with themselves, or with the doctors, even with God. "Maybe if I eat healthier, or get fitter, I can improve my chances of avoiding death," they say to themselves.

Or they tell the doctors that they'll do everything they want them to, take whatever medication, undergo any procedure or operation, anything at all as long as the treatment will ensure they live to fight another day.

Or they plea with God. "God, I'll do anything you ask, anything. Just tell me what I have to do. I'll be good. I'll go to church. I'll pray every day. I'll devote my life to worship. Just don't let me die like this."

Invariably, their bargaining and their pleading falls flat. They know in their hearts that it's all futile, that no matter what they do, no matter what treatment they have, no matter how many promises they make to God, they know with utter certainty that their death is unavoidable.

Then the black dog of depression enters the front door. This is no friendly dog, not one that you want to hug and take for walks. But it is a guard dog, a guardian of something beautiful—acceptance.

After a period of time, which is completely variable and dependent on the unique grieving journey of the patient, depression vanishes. This dark night of the soul lifts and, like a new dawn, a deep serenity settles in their heart and fills their mind with a profound peace.

Over 2,500 years ago, the Ancient Greek philosopher, Socrates, also argued that true philosophy was the practice and preparation for death. Accordingly, the true aim of philosophy was to no longer fear death, to conquer the final frontier.

Although Kübler-Ross identified the profound peace that comes from the final acceptance of one's own mortality, she repeatedly stressed that this journey to acceptance wasn't a linear journey.

Her patients didn't move in a stepwise manner from denial to anger to bargaining to depression before finally arriving at acceptance.

Rather it was a circular or spiral ascent in which many phases were experienced at once but where one phase dominated at a particular time.

The importance of understanding the grief journey is to identify which phase of grief you are currently experiencing and to learn to acknowledge and accept the situation as it is.

Acceptance of *what is* leads to peace of mind. It leads to healing. It leads to growth and advancement.

Rejection, or resistance, of what is, however, has the opposite effect: anguish, suffering, stagnation, failure to heal.

> *What you resist persists.*

This is true of anything in life. It's vital, then, that you accept whatever blocks you are experiencing.

Accepting them can be difficult. You might experience denial, you might get angry about it, even try to bargain your way out, or get depressed over it.

But if you don't accept your blocks, you are likely to remain stuck and unable to progress, unable to find peace of mind and healing.

Blocks that severely hamper and limit your ability to build effectiveness.

I: Identify the Cause

Once you have recognised the symptoms of your block and accepted that you have a block, the next step is to identify the underlying cause of the block.

One way is to use the process that doctors, nurses, and other health professionals use to identify health issues with their patients—take a history, examine the patient, request some investigations, and diagnose the illness.

Taking a history of the symptoms involves asking the right questions. What symptoms have you noticed? When did they start? What makes the symptoms worse or better? Have you or your family had these symptoms before?

The aim of taking a history from the patient is to focus on the most likely diagnoses and narrow the list of possibilities. Then the doctor will examine the patient for signs, listening to the chest, feeling for lumps and bumps, looking inside the ears and throat, inspecting the skin, and so forth.

Examination of the patient will narrow the list of possible diagnoses even further, and may even confirm the diagnosis that had been suspected when taking the history.

If the diagnosis is still up in the air, the doctor may request some investigations to build the evidence to confirm the diagnosis, such as blood tests, swabs, X-rays, and other internal imaging. Sometimes multiple investigations are needed.

Gathering all the evidence that was taken from the history, examination, and investigations, the doctor then makes a definitive or highly probable diagnosis that they then use to formulate a treatment plan for the patient.

This medical process is also a useful diagnostic tool to identify the cause of any block you might be experiencing.

First, take a history of your symptoms. When did you first notice them? Do they occur at certain times? How often do they happen? What triggers them?

Second, examine your mental and emotional state. How do your blocks make you feel? Is there a strong emotional component to your block? Why do you think this happens? You can also ask yourself what will be the consequence if your block remains and you do nothing about it?

Third, investigate which part of the brain is the dominating factor in your block, your forebrain, midbrain, or hindbrain?

Are you continually overthinking and have a forebrain block? Are you constantly overwhelmed and have a hindbrain block? Are you habitually running toward pleasurable situations, or avoiding painful situations, and have a midbrain block?

Once you have made your diagnosis and identified the cause, you can now formulate a treatment plan to help navigate your way out.

N: Navigate Your Way Out

Your life is too unique and too important to allow your blocks to limit your life and be less than what you are capable of being.

To build effectiveness is to bring meaning and value to your life and to the lives of those you touch, so it's vital that you navigate your way around your blocks and don't let them stop you being who you are and what you can be.

Remember, though, treating the symptoms is only temporary. You must treat the root cause for a permanent solution or remedy to your blocks.

Like all problems, the solution is embedded in the problem itself. You just need to look at the problem and the solution will reveal itself.

For example, if you are poor, the solution is money. If you are unwell, the solution is health. If you are unemployed, the solution is employment. Your focus then becomes a question of how to make money, how to get well, or how to get a job.

So, how do you find a solution or remedy to your blocks? You simply do the opposite!

BLOCK	REMEDY
B: Blinded by the Lights	-Delay of Gratification
L: Likes & Dislikes	-Do What's Right
O: Overthinking & Overwhelm	-Simplicity & Mindfulness
C: Cynicism & Doubt	-Embrace the Mystery (Curiosity)
K: Killjoy Attitude	-Change Perspective

TABLE 3: The 5 BLOCKs Remedy

Here are some practical tips and remedies for each of the 5 BLOCKs and some of the symptoms they may present with.

#1. <u>B: Blinded by the Lights</u>

Symptom: distraction, sensory addiction.

Cause: pleasure and pain.

Remedy: delay of gratification.

Practical Tip: The best way to navigate your way out of sensory distraction and addiction is to think of what dogs do: they *delay gratification*. They bury their bone and wait for it to ripen before digging it up and enjoying it. They are the experts in Delaying Of Gratification—D.O.G!

#2. <u>L: Likes & Dislikes</u>

Symptom: displeasure, ill will.

Cause: preferences and bias.

Remedy: do what's right despite your preferences.

Practical Tip: The best way to navigate your way out of mood motivation and ill will toward others is to think of what knights do: they *fight the good fight*. Fighting the good fight is simply doing what's right in every situation. No matter if what is happening around you is to your dislike, you have the power to always choose the right thing to do. No matter if everyone around you is behaving to your displeasure, you have the power to choose the right course of action.

#3. O: Overthinking & Overwhelm

Symptom: unable to cope.

Cause: fear of failure.

Remedy: be courageous and act despite your fear.

Practical Tip: The best way to navigate your way out of feeling overwhelmed and unable to cope is to think of what soldiers do: they are *brave under fire*. Being courageous isn't the absence of fear, it is doing what you should do despite the fears you have. This is the time to simplify and prioritise, to be mindful of the present and take each moment as it comes, even if all you can do is take one step at a time, live each hour by hour.

#4. C: Cynicism & Doubt

Symptom: futility and pointlessness.

Cause: the belief your needs won't be met.

Remedy: embrace the unknown, be curious.

Practical Tip: The best way to navigate your way out of futility and hopelessness is to think of what children do: they are *naturally curious*. Embracing the unknown is simply the attitude of being open to the mystery of life and allowing what will be to be. It is to humbly acknowledge that you don't know everything, and can't know everything, and to stop pretending that you do know everything. So let Life be your teacher, embrace the experience of today and learn from it. Greet the day with anticipation. Be vulnerable and be comfortable with being uncomfortable.

#5. <u>K: Killjoy Attitude</u>

Symptom: mental sluggishness.

Cause: lack of purpose.

Remedy: change your perspective.

Practical Tip: The best way to navigate your way out of mental sluggishness is to think of what bees do: they are energetic and positive. Why? Because they are working for *a common cause*—the well-being of the hive and the well-being of each and every bee. To feel more energetic and positive, release the shackles of your mental sluggishness by changing your perspective on why you do what you do and embracing a bigger purpose.

Q: Of the five examples just discussed, what remedy resonates with you and why? What is a practical solution to your current block?

Main Points:

1. Let it RAIN: Recognise the symptoms of your block; Accept you have a block; Identify the cause of your block; Navigate your way out.
2. Like all problems, the solution is embedded in the problem itself.
3. You can find a solution or remedy to your blocks by simply doing the opposite!

PART **2**

STRATEGIES

FOR A MORE

EFFECTIVE

MINDSET

6 EFFECTIVE SELF-MANAGEMENT

'Don't wish it were easier, wish you were better.'
Jim Rohn

THE KEY TO unlocking an effective mindset is self-management. Mindset, as we know, is one of the three vital elements of The Effectiveness Equation, $E = MC^2$, where capability and capacity are the other vital elements.

Building our effectiveness is how we will break free from our self-imposed limitations and escape the flea circus.

But to improve our effectiveness, we first need to improve our mindset; and to improve our mindset, we need to improve our self-management. Therefore, improving our self-management will improve our effectiveness.

The remaining chapters of this guidebook will now focus on the more practical aspects of how to improve our mindset, as well as strategies to improve our capability and capacity.

Even the implementation of just one of the strategies we will be discussing will successfully increase your effectiveness, but for now we will concentrate on improving your mindset through good self-management. After this, *Part 3* will be dedicated to discussing the strategies to improve your capability and capacity, in particular energy-management, time-management, and goal-setting.

DEFINING SELF-MANAGEMENT

According to psychologists, there are four requirements you will need to embrace to exhibit good self-management. They are:

1. Responsible choice-making.
2. Mature reasoning and emotional intelligence.
3. Self-determination.
4. Self-leadership.

To exhibit good self-management, and thus exhibit an effective mindset, you will need to show responsible choice-making, which is the ability to make reasonable and informed decisions.

You will need to show mature reasoning and emotional intelligence, which is the ability to control your own actions and emotions.

You will need to show self-determination, which is the ability to set and achieve personal and professional goals

You will also need to show self-leadership, which is the ability to be a positive influence for yourself and in your environment.

Daniel Goleman, bestselling author of *Emotional Intelligence*, has defined self-management as:[8]

> *Being able to manage impulses and moods and to think before acting.*

---

[8] Daniel Goleman, What makes a leader? *Harvard Business Review*, 1998

We will use this definition in discussing strategies for self-management, emphasising the importance of managing impulses (natural instincts), moods (emotions), and thinking (thoughts), the same three filters of awareness and blocks to effectiveness we have so far been discussing.

IDENTIFYING SELF-MANAGEMENT AREAS OF NEED

In order to work on and improve your self-management, and thus your effectiveness, you will need to identify areas of need.

As such, we will focus on two main areas. In the next four chapters, we will focus on the first area of need, which is identifying self-limiting *habits* and implementing the strategies to overcome these habits. Following this, we will focus on the second area of need, identifying self-limiting *thoughts* and implementing the strategies to overcome these thoughts.

The below table is a summary of common self-limiting behaviours amongst many people.

SELF-LIMITING BEHAVIOURS	
Not starting things.	Not finishing things.
Poor preparation.	Inability to commit.
Failure to follow through.	Failure to follow up.
Putting yourself/others down.	Not putting yourself forward.
Controlling behaviour.	Poor listening, talking too much.
Avoid difficult things, give up.	Not asking for help.

TABLE 4:   Self-Limiting Behaviours

Q: Of the self-limiting behaviours just listed, what behaviours resonate with you and why? What is the result of these behaviours? What is the true cost of continuing these behaviours and not doing anything about them?

The problem with repeating these self-limiting behaviours over and over again, even for many years, is that they become entrenched as self-limiting habits; and the problem with self-limiting habits is that your effectiveness becomes self-limiting.

As the old proverb goes:

Sow a thought, you reap an act.
Sow an act, you reap a habit.
Sow a habit, you reap a character.
Sow a character, you reap a destiny.

We will now discuss four self-limiting habits that arise from constant repetition of self-limiting behaviours and the strategies you can use to overcome them to develop positive habits and build your effectiveness:

1. Inability to say 'no'.

2. Procrastination.

3. Approval seeking.

4. Perfectionism.

Main Points:

1. The key to unlocking an effective mindset is self-management.
2. Building our effectiveness is how we will break free from our self-imposed limitations and escape the flea circus.
3. Self-management is being able to manage impulses and moods and to think before acting.
4. The problem with self-limiting habits is that your effectiveness becomes self-limiting.
5. Sow a thought, you reap an act.

7 INABILITY TO SAY 'NO'

'The difference between successful people and really
successful people is that really successful people say
no to almost everything.'

Warren Buffet

IN OUR PERSONAL and professional life, the ability to say
'no' is as critical as saying 'yes'. However, it always surprises me
how many of my clients struggle with the inability to utter this
simple word.

On the surface, this probably doesn't seem too much of a
problem. But its effects are often hidden and insidious. The
inability to say 'no' can have far-reaching effects that hinder
your productivity, stifle creativity, and even lead to burnout.

> *The inability to say 'no' is often rooted in a need
> to please others, a desire to avoid conflict, or a
> fear of missing out on opportunities.*

A need to please others is common. You may feel that
consistently accommodating requests and taking on additional
responsibilities will earn you the respect and admiration from
others, such as partners, colleagues, superiors, or clients.

But this desire to be a team player or a people-pleaser can
quickly develop into an overwhelming burden.

The desire to avoid conflict is another common reason for not saying 'no'. The mere thought of disappointing others or potentially causing friction is paralysing for some people.

The easiest thing to avoid conflict is to take the path of least resistance, agreeing to every request from family or colleagues, piling on more tasks, all to avoid uncomfortable conversations or disagreements.

Unfortunately, the desire to avoid conflict, while seemingly harmless, can lead to many unforeseen problems down the line, which we'll soon discuss in *Consequences of Not Saying 'No'*.

The fear of missing out on opportunities is also a powerful motivator for some. You might find it difficult to turn down new projects, assignments, or collaborations at work, fearing that saying 'no' might result in a missed opportunity for a promotion or other career advancement.

> Q: What are the reasons you can't say 'no' that get in the way of reaching your professional or personal goals or being effective?
>
> -> Approval seeking?
>
> -> You think you should?
>
> -> You need control?
>
> -> You think you are indispensable?
>
> -> You want to be the centre of attention?
>
> -> You don't want to offend?
>
> -> Other?

Consequences of Not Saying 'No'

The inability to say 'no', however, is a double-edged sword.

While on the surface it may seem well-intentioned and solve immediate problems, the inability to say 'no', or always saying 'yes', can severely limit your effectiveness and lead to some unintended consequences.

We will now discuss some examples of how this issue can lead to negative effects:

1. Overcommitment.
2. Work-Life Imbalance.
3. Weakened Boundaries.
4. Reduced Creativity and Innovation.

#1: Overcommitment

Overcommitment and a lack of focus can severely impact your effectiveness because those who struggle to say 'no' often become overloaded with tasks and projects.

When individuals stretch themselves too thin, they fail to perform at their best, which can lead to substandard work, missed deadlines, and stress, which ultimately result in diminished productivity.

What's more, every 'yes' comes with an implicit opportunity cost. By taking on tasks that don't necessarily align with your skills, interests, or long-term goals, you risk missing out on opportunities that could genuinely enhance your personal or professional development.

#2: Work-Life Imbalance

A healthy work-life balance is essential for overall personal development and well-being.

However, an inability to say 'no' can lead to excessive overtime and/or bringing work home after hours and on the weekends.

The blurring of the line between work and personal life erodes work-life balance and results in strained personal relationships and exhaustion.

Unchecked, this constant workload and always being 'on' 24 hours a day without 'switching off' increases your risk of chronic stress, burnout, and decreased job satisfaction.

Burnout, although not a diagnosed condition as such, can result from periods of long-term stress, and is characterised by a "combination of feeling exhausted, feeling negative about (or less connected to) the work or activity you're doing, and a feeling of reduced performance".[9]

An important component of preventing burnout is the ability to 'switch off' and give your mind and body regular downtime to relax, recuperate, and re-energise. You owe it to your work, your family, and most importantly to yourself.

Crucial to 'switching off' is the ability to say 'no' and the discipline to keep saying it.

---

[9] Beyond Blue, www.beyondblue.org.au

#3: Weakened Boundaries

When people constantly say 'yes,' they risk sacrificing their boundaries by accepting responsibilities that aren't aligned with their skills, expertise, or goals, with the direct result of limiting their effectiveness.

While it may seem like a quick fix in the short term, over time, the inability to say 'no' results in poor quality work, missed opportunities for learning and growth, and potential harm to your professional reputation.

For instance, an individual who is a marketing expert taking on a complex IT project may produce substandard results, leading to frustration and dissatisfaction for both the individual and her bosses.

What's more, without the ability to discern between what aligns with your career goals and what doesn't, you can easily find yourself on a trajectory that is far from your intended destination.

This can lead to a lack of job satisfaction, disengagement, and feeling unfulfilled in your career. If it goes on for long enough, the habit of accepting projects that do not contribute to your professional goals can result in feelings of stagnation and loss of confidence, even lost opportunities for advancement.

#4: Reduced Creativity and Innovation

When individuals find themselves stretched too thin due to an inability to say 'no,' it creates a stifling environment for creativity and innovation.

Creativity and innovation thrive in a relaxed state of mind during periods of downtime when the mind is free to wander, which is practically impossible when you are inundated with tasks.

When overcommitted, you rarely have the luxury of such downtime. If your schedule is packed from morning to night, any semblance of leisure or relaxation is scarce. Without this respite, your mind doesn't have the opportunity to process and synthesise new ideas.

This is because your mental capacity is compromised when constantly preoccupied with the demands of existing responsibilities and swamped with an excessive workload. When consumed by managing tasks and meeting deadlines, it leaves very little bandwidth for creative thinking and problem-solving.

In a work environment, creative solutions often emerge from the cross-pollination of ideas, but this is hindered when overcommitment isolates team members.

In such an environment where everyone is overwhelmed with tasks and team members struggle to keep up with their individual workloads, brainstorming sessions and knowledge-sharing opportunities become less frequent and collaboration often takes a backseat.

Overcommitted individuals and teams also become risk-averse. With little time and energy to spare, they tend to opt for safe and conventional solutions rather than thinking outside the box to explore more innovative or unconventional approaches.

What's more, when you are stretched so thin that any setbacks can lead to severe consequences, the fear of failure intensifies, further isolating yourself and lessening collaboration with others.

This also has knock-on effects to your overall sense of well-being, because when you are unable to unleash your creative potential due to overcommitment, job satisfaction declines, leading to disengagement with your work and decreased motivation.

Q: What are some consequences that not saying 'no' has had that stopped you from being effective in your 7 Life Segments?

-> Family & Relationships?

-> Career & Work?

-> Money & Finances?

-> Health & Wellbeing?

-> Learning & Education?

-> Fun & Adventure?

-> Spirituality & Ethics?

Strategies for Effectively Saying 'No'

Clear communication and a positive approach to problem-solving are key when it comes to saying 'no'.

Here are some strategies that clients of mine have successfully used, and I myself often use, that you might find useful for saying 'no' at home and at work.

By employing these strategies, you can assert your boundaries, maintain the quality of your work, and promote a collaborative environment in which alternative solutions are sought when necessary.

1. Evaluate the Situation.
2. Communicate Your Constraints.
3. Avoid Making Excuses.
4. Employ the 80/20 Rule.
5. Negotiate Where Possible.
6. Maintain a Positive Tone.
7. Practice Assertiveness.
8. Prioritise Self-Care.

#1: Evaluate the Situation

Consider the context and urgency of the request. When you're approached with additional tasks and you're already operating at full capacity, it's essential to assess the implications.

> Tip: If taking on more work would compromise the quality of your existing responsibilities or increase the likelihood of failure, it's time to say 'no'.

#2: Communicate Your Constraints

Instead of outright declining the request, explain the difficulties it would pose.

> Tip: You have the right to be transparent about your limitations.

For instance, you can say, "If you would like me to take on this task, I will need to let go of task A, B, or C, get more resources, or extend time frames."

This demonstrates your commitment to maintaining quality and ensures that your boundaries are clear.

#3: Avoid Making Excuses

While explaining your constraints, it's important not to make excuses or provide unnecessary justifications.

Tip: Keep your response concise and to the point.

Don't give hundreds of reasons why you can't. Over-explaining can dilute your message and make it seem like you're uncertain about your decision.

#4: Employ the 80/20 Rule

Your 'no' should be succinct, followed by a brief explanation of why you can't accommodate the request (20%).

Tip: The majority of your response (80%) should focus on providing alternate solutions to the problem that don't involve you.

This 80/20 approach shows that you are committed to helping find a resolution, even if you can't be directly involved.

#5: Negotiate When Possible

In some cases, you may be able to negotiate with the requester.

> Tip: Discuss the possibility of delegating the task to someone else or extending the time frame to make it more manageable.

This demonstrates your willingness to be a team player while still maintaining your boundaries.

#6: Maintain a Positive Tone

It's important to maintain a respectful and positive tone throughout the conversation.

> Tip: Emphasise that your decision is driven by a commitment to delivering quality work, and that you're open to collaborating on alternative solutions.

#7: Practice Assertiveness

Assertiveness is a valuable skill when saying 'no.' It's about confidently and respectfully standing your ground.

> Tip: Practice saying 'no' in a firm but polite manner to strengthen your ability to do so in professional situations.

#8: Prioritise Self-Care

Recognise the importance of maintaining a balance between work and personal life (as discussed in *Work-Life Imbalance*).

Tip: Saying 'no' when necessary is a crucial aspect of self-care, ensuring that you can perform at your best and maintain overall well-being.

Will You Say 'No'?

When implementing these strategies on saying 'no' at home and in the workplace, it will benefit you to remember these points:

-> Get clarity on what is important to you, your priorities, your purpose, in both your personal and professional life.

-> Do not respond to a request immediately—give yourself time to think whether you want/are able to do it.

-> Understand your need to say 'yes' all the time.

-> Practice makes perfect.

-> Say no to the small things and build up your confidence.

-> Practice saying: "Thanks for asking me... I'll let you know on (date/time) if I can do it."

Now go out and try it. You'll be amazed at how using this simple word 'no' in an appropriate way will boost your confidence, clear your mind, and build your effectiveness.

Main Points:

1. The inability to say 'no' is often rooted in a need to please others, a desire to avoid conflict, or a fear of missing out on opportunities.
2. The ability to say 'no' is as critical as saying 'yes'.
3. Those who struggle to say 'no' often become overloaded with tasks and projects and stretch themselves thin.
4. A healthy work-life balance is essential for overall personal development and well-being.
5. When people constantly say 'yes,' they risk sacrificing their boundaries by accepting responsibilities that aren't aligned with their skills, expertise, or goals.
6. Creativity and innovation thrive in a relaxed state of mind during periods of downtime when the mind is free to wander.
7. Clear communication and a positive approach to problem-solving are key when it comes to saying 'no.'

8 BREAKING THROUGH PROCRASTINATION

'While wasting our time hesitating and procrastinating, life goes on.'

Seneca

IN THE INTRODUCTION we mentioned how we often overestimate what we can accomplish in a single day and underestimate what we can achieve over a lifetime.

But what holds many of us back from realising our true potential and limits our success is the all-too-common act of procrastination.

> *Procrastination is characterised by the irrational inclination to defer essential tasks and obligations, even when fully aware of the adverse consequences that such delays can have on both individuals and the entities they are associated with.*

The truth is, most of us engage in procrastination at some point, often putting off tasks we know we should tackle.

While procrastination may be considered a normal part of human behaviour, what is far from normal is allowing procrastination to persist for years on end.

Unfortunately, this is the reality for approximately 20-25% of individuals,[10] and the repercussions are extensive, impacting both individuals and society at large.

We currently live in a fascinating era where instant information is readily available at our fingertips, thanks to the rapid advancements in technology. Yet, the downside is that this constant influx of information can leave us feeling overwhelmed and inundated.

Studies have shown that stress levels surged by up to 30% within three decades from the 1980s, and that chronic procrastination increased nearly fivefold since the 1970s.

What's more, as we discussed in *The RETAINED Model*[TM], a staggering 85% of employees are disengaged at work, meaning only one in six workers at any given time are genuinely committed to their tasks and not procrastinating.

> *Procrastination has the potential to not only disrupt individual lives but to also disrupt businesses and national finances.*

Q: What situations do you procrastinate? How long has this been happening? Does procrastination get in the way of reaching your professional or personal goals or being effective?

---

[10] Piers Steel, The nature of procrastination: a meta-analytic and theoretical review of quintessential self-regulatory failure. *Psychological Buletin*, 2007

Consequences of Procrastination

Reflecting on my younger years, I too was a chronic procrastinator. For over a decade, I constantly pushed back my dream of writing a book. Despite a deep passion for reading and an abundance of stories I wanted to share, I perpetually found reasons for not starting.

Whether it was being too busy, too engrossed in studies, too preoccupied with social activities, or having too little time, my favourite excuse I ended up using for many years was, "I don't have a computer."

In the mid-90s, that was a valid excuse. Computers weren't the everyday household item they are today, and they were relatively expensive.

But the problem wasn't the lack of a home computer, or my ability to afford one, it was me. I had effectively postponed my dream of writing a book for over half my life, proving to everyone, including myself, that I was more of a 'gunna' than a 'doer'. I had become the Professor of Procrastination.

The problem with procrastination is that it surreptitiously steals your precious time, leaving little room to live the life you truly desire. That's why it's called 'The Thief of Time', and why I call it 'The Killer of Dreams'.

It was only after enduring years of procrastination that I came to grasp a fundamental life lesson:

What you think about, you become.

If you think you don't have the know-how or the skills or the tools or the time or the money to achieve what you want to achieve, or you think you're not clever enough to do what you want to do, then that becomes the world in which you live out your life. Just like I had.

In other words, your thoughts and beliefs shape your actions and, consequently, your reality. With your thoughts you create your world. What you focus on, you experience.

> Q: What are some of the consequences that procrastination has had that stopped you from being effective in your 7 Life Segments?
>
> -> Family & Relationships?
>
> -> Career & Work?
>
> -> Money & Finances?
>
> -> Health & Wellbeing?
>
> -> Learning & Education?
>
> -> Fun & Adventure?
>
> -> Spirituality & Ethics?

Strategies for Procrastination

An ounce of action is worth a pound of theorising, as life coaches like to say. While thinking and planning is vitally important, it is action that brings our dreams and plans to fruition. It is action that propels us forward, opening the doors to opportunities.

We will now discuss four strategies to defeat procrastination so you can take action and build your effectiveness:

1. Identify excuses preventing you from taking action.

2. Identify a fear preventing you from taking action.

3. Identify a reward for taking action.

4. Identify a value 'motivation' for taking action.

#1: Identify Excuses

Excuse-making is a common human tendency that often goes unnoticed, yet it can have a profound impact on our personal and professional effectiveness. By continually making excuses, we create barriers to success, hinder our growth, and limit our potential.

> *At its core, excuse-making is the act of providing justifications, rationalisations, or explanations for why we couldn't, shouldn't, or didn't do something we initially intended to do.*

Excuse-making is a self-imposed obstacle to our effectiveness. While some excuses may appear valid, they often mask underlying fears, insecurities, or a lack of commitment.

This habit can manifest in various forms, one of which is procrastination. We convince ourselves that we can't start a task or project now due to various reasons, postponing it indefinitely.

One of the problems with excuse-making is the unhelpful conclusions we draw from our excuses. These unhelpful conclusions reinforce the initial excuse, which in turn reinforces the procrastinating behaviour.

For instance, the excuse, "I don't want to do it now," leads to the unhelpful conclusion, "I might feel more like doing it tomorrow." Which, of course, you probably won't.

Below is a table of excuses and the unhelpful conclusions that we draw from them.

EXCUSES	UNHELPFUL CONCLUSIONS
I'm really tired.	I am better off doing it after I have rested.
I don't want to do it now.	I might feel more like doing it tomorrow.
I'll miss out on all the fun (FOMO).	I can always wait until nothing is happening.
I don't have everything I need.	I will wait until I have everything I need.
I have plenty of time.	So I don't have to start now.
I don't feel inspired / I'm not in the mood.	I'll wait until I am.
I have other things to do.	I will do it once those things are finished.

TABLE 5: Excuses & Unhelpful Conclusions

Q: Do any of these excuses and unhelpful conclusions resonate with you? What are some unhelpful conclusions you draw from the excuses you make?

To combat excuse-making and their unhelpful conclusions, you must first be alert to when you are thinking and offering excuses.

Then, focus on replacing these excuses with constructive solutions that turn an unhelpful conclusion into a helpful conclusion.

You do this by inserting a powerful, but simple, three-letter word after a negative statement or unhelpful conclusion—BUT!

> *The word 'but' has the power to not only change negative thoughts and words into positive thoughts and words, but has the power to transform your life into abundance and joy.*

I call this strategy 'Inserting the But', and it is one of the most powerful strategies you can use to break free from not just this limiting habit of excuse-making, but almost any self-limiting belief that is holding you back.

EXCUSES	HELPFUL CONCLUSIONS
I'm really tired.	BUT... I can make a small start now and then rest.
I don't want to do it now.	BUT... later won't be any better, so I may as well start.
I'll miss out on all the fun (FOMO).	BUT... if I get some done, I can reward myself later.
I don't have everything I need.	BUT... I can still try to make a start on some of the task.
I have plenty of time.	BUT... better to get on top of it now than leave it.
I don't feel inspired / I'm not in the mood.	BUT... if I get started, the inspiration will follow.
I have other things to do.	BUT... they are not more important and can wait.

TABLE 6: 'Inserting the But' & Helpful Conclusions

Kylie T. is a client of mine who testifies to the power of 'Inserting the But'. When Kylie first began to attend my coaching sessions, she was working in the finance industry but was considering a career change. She was nervous about taking the leap and had a lot of negative thoughts about herself.

But within days of implementing the strategy of 'Inserting the But', she saw an almost immediate improvement in her confidence and mental well-being.

One month later, she said to me: "Since I met you, I feel like I'm living in a world of abundance."

This strategy really is that powerful.

> Q: Consider the excuses you have been making and their unhelpful conclusions. How can you change them into more helpful conclusions by 'Inserting the But'?

#2: Identify a Fear

Fear is an ever-present and often invisible force that wields significant influence over our lives. When it comes to effectiveness and success, fear is one of the biggest obstacles we face.

Procrastination is a direct offspring of fear. It thrives on our hesitation, hesitation fueled by various fears—fear of failure, fear of rejection, fear of the unknown, and sometimes even the fear of success.

These fears, while natural, can become debilitating. They can paralyse us and prevent us from taking action to achieve our goals.

As bestselling author of *Chicken Soup for the Soul*, Jack Canfield, said:[11]

> *Fear is the main reason people procrastinate... So we play it safe and avoid taking risks or trying new things.*

It's therefore vital to understand that our potential for success and personal growth lies on the other side of our fears.

---

[11] Jack Canfield and Mark Hansen, *Chicken Soup for the Soul*, HCI, 1993

Q: What fears get in the way of reaching your professional or personal goals or being effective?

The consequences of fear are many and varied. Here are some examples:

Self-Doubt

Fear often fuels self-doubt, making us question our abilities and judgement. This self-doubt is like a heavy weight that holds us back from taking action.

Risk Aversion

The fear of failure or fear of rejection can lead to risk aversion. We become unwilling to step out of our comfort zones and try something new or challenging, even if it promises growth and success.

Analysis Paralysis

Fear can also push us into a cycle of overthinking and analysis paralysis. We become so engrossed in the 'what-ifs' and potential negative outcomes that we find it difficult to make decisions, let alone take action.

Avoidance Behaviour

Fear is a big trigger of avoidance behaviour. We procrastinate because we actively avoid confronting our fears, and in doing so, we inadvertently stifle our effectiveness.

Opportunity Cost

Every moment we spend procrastinating due to fear represents an opportunity cost. We waste time that could be invested in personal and professional growth, creativity, and achievement.

So, what can we do to break free from the shackles of fear and conquer procrastination?

By understanding, accepting, and actively acknowledging our fears. As Mahatma Gandhi said:

To do what we fear is the first step to success.

Confronting your fears may appear daunting at first. But in my own experience, I was only able to break free from the cycle of procrastination when I realised it was my own fear of rejection that had prevented me from writing the books I had always dreamed of writing.

It was only after I fully understood my fear of rejection and my need to be accepted by everyone, when I accepted that this fear was preventing me from typing the first words of my book, and when I acknowledged that this fear was also pervasive in many other aspects of my life, that I was able to face down this fear and take the leap of faith I had avoided taking for half my life.

If I hadn't confronted my fear, I would not be able to help others with their fears, and you would not be reading this guidebook. Which, by the way, is my tenth book, and I have plans for at least thirty more. For good or for bad, the floodgates have opened.

So here are some simple strategies that will help you tackle your fears and break free from procrastination:

Awareness

The first step is to recognise your fears and understand how they manifest as procrastination. Self-awareness is vital to overcoming this obstacle.

Acceptance

Accept that fear is a natural part of the human experience. It's okay to feel fear, but it's not okay to let it control your actions.

Setting Clear Goals

Establish clear, achievable goals and break them down into manageable steps. Smaller, more achievable tasks are less intimidating, making it easier to overcome fear and take action (see *Chapter 14: Effective Goal-Setting* for more details).

Effective Self-Talk

Cultivate a habit of positive self-talk. Here you can use the strategy of 'Inserting the But' that we discussed previously. Use the 'But' to mitigate self-doubt and replace negative thoughts with positive statements that reinforce your capabilities (see *Chapter 11: Effective Self-Talk* for more details).

Seek Support

Don't be afraid to seek the support from friends, mentors, or coaches. Having someone to help you face your fears and encourage you to take action can be a powerful way to break through procrastinating habits.

The path to success is through fear, but it is a path worth traversing for it is on the other side of your fear that your greatest achievements and personal growth await.

As Richard Bach, bestselling author of *Jonathan Livingston Seagull*,[12] said:

> *Overcome fear, behold wonder.*

---

[12] Richard Bach, *Jonathan Livingston Seagull*, Scribner 1970

Q: Consider any fears that have caused you to procrastinate and limited your effectiveness. How can you redefine those fears into more helpful motivators?

#3: Identify a Reward

In our discussion on the 5 BLOCKs, we mentioned two types of distraction: arousal and avoidance.

Arousal distraction occurs when you intentionally divert your attention away from your current or pending tasks by engaging in more enjoyable or effortless activities. This typically involves succumbing to the temptation of seeking immediate gratification.

For example, instead of attending to household chores like washing the dishes or vacuuming the floor, you might opt to indulge in watching TV or playing computer games. At work, instead of tackling essential tasks like drafting a business proposal or submitting your monthly report, you find yourself drawn to activities like social media or gossiping with others.

Avoidance distraction is the intentional act of engaging in alternative tasks, deliberately diverting your attention from a pressing obligation that you don't want to face.

Avoidance distraction is driven by the desire to evade the discomfort associated with tasks that demand emotional, intellectual, or physical exertion.

Both types of distraction involve the pleasure and pain area of your brain, the paleomammalian midbrain. Pleasure triggers arousal distraction, and pain triggers avoidance distraction.

Unfortunately, procrastination often finds its roots in the interplay between pleasure and pain. Which is why it's essential to understand how these powerful motivators affect your behaviour, as they can either propel you toward success or keep you mired in failure.

> Q: What is a pleasure (desire) or a pain that gets in the way of reaching your professional or personal goals or being effective?

Of themselves, pleasure and pain are everyday, normal human experiences. Issues arise, however, when habits of arousal and avoidance distraction limit our effectiveness.

Here are some examples of how the forces of pleasure and pain interact to cause procrastination:

The Pleasure of Distraction

One of the most common forms of pleasure that triggers procrastination is the allure of distraction. Pleasure, in the context of procrastination, represents immediate gratification. It lures us away from our tasks and tempts us with the allure of comfort and instant satisfaction. This provides a temporary respite from unwanted tasks but ultimately undermines our effectiveness.

The Pain of the Task

Procrastination also arises from the fear of pain or discomfort associated with the task at hand. It's the emotional and mental resistance we feel when confronted with challenging or undesirable work. If a task requires substantial mental, emotional or physical effort, we may find ourselves procrastinating to escape the discomfort of starting or completing it.

What's more, if a project seems daunting, monotonous, or unenjoyable, we naturally gravitate toward tasks that promise more immediate pleasure, even if they aren't conducive to our ultimate objectives.

Instant vs Delayed Gratification

The tug-of-war between short-term and long-term gratification is a central theme in procrastination. Pleasure can be derived from postponing tasks, as we opt for instant satisfaction over the delayed reward of finishing our tasks and completing our goals. This decision, however, often leads to missed opportunities, increased stress, and reduced effectiveness in the long run.

* * *

So, how can you navigate the complex terrain of pleasure and pain to overcome procrastination and build your effectiveness?

Ultimately, it is the conscious choices you make that will determine whether you succumb to whims of pleasure and pain or power forward with effective action.

So, this is what you can do. First, recognise when the arousal/avoidance dynamic is at play when procrastination strikes. Self-awareness is the first step in nullifying the effects of this dynamic.

Then employ some or all of these strategies listed below to minimise the impact of arousal and avoidant distraction. These strategies are designed to counteract the negative influence of your paleomammalian midbrain by offering rewards that are longer lasting than the fleeting sugar hit of procrastinating habits.

Goal Setting

Establish clear, achievable goals with specific deadlines. This creates a sense of purpose and a vision for the future, diluting the allure of short-term pleasures. Multiply the benefits of this strategy by setting short- and long-term goals in each of your 7 Life Segments (see *Chapter 14: Effective Goal-Setting* for more details).

Break Tasks Down

How do you eat an elephant? One bite at a time. By dividing larger, daunting tasks into smaller, more manageable components and tackling them in bite-sized portions, you can negate any feelings of overwhelm and minimise the perceived pain associated with the task.

Find Intrinsic Motivation

Seek intrinsic motivation in your tasks by focusing on the personal satisfaction and long-term rewards that accomplishing them will bring. Shift your perspective from the pain of the process to the pleasure of the outcome.

Embrace Discomfort

Bodybuilders and butterflies know that discomfort is a natural part of growth. Without the effort and strain of working out in the gym, muscles won't grow. Without the dissolving and reassembly of the caterpillar's body in the chrysalis, the new wings of the butterfly will not develop.

By embracing discomfort, you can prevent its paralysing effect with the knowledge that your future reward is dependent on what you are doing in this moment.

Delay Gratification

Dogs are masters at delaying gratification, which is the art of postponing immediate rewards or pleasures in pursuit of long-term goals and greater success. Dogs bury their bones and wait for them to ripen under the soil for a more enjoyable meal at a later date.

Although it requires self-discipline, patience, and the ability to resist the temptation of instant pleasure for the sake of more significant, future achievements, delaying gratification is a guaranteed way of beating procrastination and maximising your sense of enjoyment in life.

> Q: Consider any distractions that have caused you to procrastinate and limited your effectiveness. How can you reward yourself to better motivate yourself to take action?

4: Identify a Value

Values serve as the moral compass of our lives, influencing the choices we make and the direction we take. They are a collection of guiding principles that determine what we deem as correct and desirable.

> *When you consistently honour your values through living them, you experience fulfilment and a heightened quality of life. You experience less stress and greater peace of mind. You experience greater harmony between who you are being and what you are doing. You experience greater effectiveness.*

Values can be divided into three categories: Personal, Core, and Community. For instance, honesty, integrity, and humility are personal values. Goodness, Truth and Beauty are core values, and liberty, diversity, and freedom of speech are community values.

Table 7 lists some values and shows how they are arranged in these three categories. There are hundreds, if not thousands, of values, so this table only represents a handful that you can choose from.

Personal values are those values you believe best suit yourself. They are the ideals, the beliefs, the principles to which you hold as a standard to live up to. They determine how you see yourself as a person, as an individual, as a human being.

Community values are those values you believe best suit the local and national community in which you live. They are the rules, the philosophies, the rights to which you agree to live by in accordance with the laws of the land. They determine how you see yourself as a community, as a nation, as a culture.

Core Values unite your community and personal values.

PERSONAL VALUE	CORE VALUE	COMMUNITY VALUE
Selflessness and courage	GOODNESS	Tolerance
Charity and gratitude		Democracy
Fairness and forgiveness		Fraternity
Religion and spirituality		Religious freedom
Honesty and humility	TRUTH	Justice
Wisdom and patience		Rule of law
Purpose and meaning		Freedom of speech
Self-Leadership and discipline		Right to life/ Human rights
Love and kindness	BEAUTY	Liberty
Appreciation of beauty and Love of learning		Equality
Humour and hope		Inclusivity
Passion and creativity		Diversity

TABLE 7: Personal, Core & Community Values

If community values and personal values are two ends of a bow tie, then Core Values are the knot in the middle. Core Values are the thread from which all other values are woven.

Although there are thousands of community and personal values, there are only three Core Values: Goodness, Truth, and Beauty.

> *Goodness, Truth & Beauty are Principle, that which is absolute and non-dual, without opposite. They are unbreakable Laws of the Universe, the founding principles from which all life is governed.*

Procrastination, however, often embeds in the misalignment between our actions and our values. To break free from the shackles of procrastination, it's imperative to recognise, rekindle, and embrace the values that you wish to embody and express.

> Q: What is a personal, core or community value that you may have forgotten or ignored that has hindered you reaching your professional or personal goals or being effective?

For instance, one such personal value that frequently goes neglected is 'discipline'. Discipline is the ability to control your behaviour in a way that leads to increased productivity and/or better habits

When discipline is a central tenet of your value system, you inherently understand the importance of structure and self-control in achieving personal and professional goals.

But misalignment can occur when you are tempted to veer off course from your disciplined path, for example, by arousal distraction. By reinforcing your connection to the value of discipline, however, you can transform your discipline into a potent source of motivation.

Instead of succumbing to procrastination, you can remind yourself of your unwavering commitment to disciplined action, thus staying the course and continuing to take the necessary action to achieve your goals.

Another value is the 'love of learning', or self-improvement. This value reflects your desire for personal growth, lifelong learning, and continual evolution.

If, however, the need for instant gratification hinders your path to self-improvement, you will likely feel an incongruency between your aspirations and your emotions, causing you to procrastinate.

Acknowledging the value of self-improvement and its future benefits can reinvigorate your efforts to do the work of personal growth. The pursuit of knowledge, personal development, peace and happiness, and the realisation of your potential can negate the false promises of procrastination.

'Integrity' is also a value that lies at the heart of many of our belief systems. Unfortunately, if you are tempted to procrastinate, you actually compromise your integrity because you fail to honour your commitments.

Reconnecting with your values of honesty and integrity can reinforce your sense of duty and responsibility, which you can then instill into your actions. By doing what you say you will, you not only regain your integrity but also disengage the machinery of procrastination.

'Gratitude' too is a powerful tool to counter procrastination. It is a reminder to appreciate the present moment and the opportunities it holds. When procrastination threatens to steal your precious time, reflecting on the value of gratitude can trigger positive action through the recognition of the preciousness of each moment.

Ultimately, the key to overcoming procrastination lies in the alignment of your actions with your values.

> *Values are not merely guiding principles; they are the driving force that can transform procrastination into productivity, bringing you closer to the fulfillment of your dreams and the realisation of your full potential.*

Q: Consider any neglect of values that have caused you to procrastinate and limited your effectiveness. How can you use personal, core, or community values to better motivate yourself to take action?

Main Points:

1. Procrastination, the 'Thief of Time', is characterised by the irrational inclination to defer essential tasks and obligations.
2. What you think about, you become.
3. One of the problems with excuse-making is the unhelpful conclusions we draw from our excuses.
4. 'Inserting the But' is one of the most powerful strategies you can use to break free from excuse-making and almost any self-limiting belief.
5. Fear is the main reason people procrastinate.
6. To do what we fear is the first step to success.
7. Procrastination often finds its roots in the interplay between pleasure and pain.
8. The conscious choices you make determine whether you succumb to whims of pleasure and pain or power forward with effective action.
9. When you consistently honour your values through living them, you experience fulfilment and a heightened quality of life.
10. Values can be divided into three categories: Personal, Core, and Community.
11. Procrastination often embeds in the misalignment between our actions and our values.
12. The key to overcoming procrastination lies in the alignment of your actions with your values.
13. Values are not merely guiding principles; they are the driving force that can transform procrastination into productivity.

9 PRIORITISING SELF-APPROVAL

'Remind yourself that you cannot fail at being yourself.'
Wayne Dyer

IN A WORLD that puts a lot of emphasis on external validation and instant likeability, the concept of self-approval might seem somewhat unconventional. However, self-approval is a potent source of personal empowerment that can transform our lives in significant ways.

Self-approval is an essential building block of our mental and emotional well-being. It's the foundation on which our confidence, self-worth, and well-being are built, ultimately shaping how we perceive and interact with the world around us.

Self-approval is the act of recognising, acknowledging, and validating ourselves independently of external opinions, judgements, or validation. It involves embracing our self-worth, our abilities, and our intrinsic value, thereby promoting a positive self-image and a sense of self-acceptance.

Self-approval is an essential component of personal well-being. It signifies the capacity to trust our own judgements, decisions, and actions, free from the relentless need for external validation.

Self-approval is like an internal safehouse, a secure inner sanctum where we are free to be our authentic self, a place in which we can relax with total self-acceptance and independence from the opinions of others.

Through self-approval, we gain the inner confidence to face life's challenges, build genuine connections, and pursue our dreams with unwavering belief in our purpose and abilities.

Self-approval is therefore a cornerstone of a fulfilling and successful life. With it, we are empowered to lead a life true to ourselves and our own values.

Without it, however, we become inauthentic, needy, and ineffective.

Approval-Seeking Behaviour

Self-approval, unfortunately, is a rare commodity. Studies have shown that up to 85% of people worldwide, adults and adolescents, have issues with self-approval.[13]

This means that every time you enter a place where people have gathered, whether socially or at work, only one in six of those people in that gathering has a strong sense of self-approval.

The remaining five out of six have a low sense of self-approval. They don't like the way they look, they think others don't like them, they make negative comparisons with other people, they have a gloomy view of their future, they are critical of themselves, they see themselves as weak and powerless, and they are generally unhappy with the cards life has dealt them.

[13] Psychology Today, 2019

The issue with low self-approval is that it gives rise to a persistently pessimistic outlook that infiltrates our thought processes, which potentially drives self-destructive patterns of behaviour and a range of mental health concerns.

Low self-approval is, as researchers have shown, associated with a number of societal issues, including high dropout rates at school, violent behaviour, elevated suicide rates, teenage pregnancy, and academic underachievement.

Although these behaviours are the extreme consequences of low self-approval, it can still cause dysfunctional behaviour that limits our day-to-day effectiveness.

Approval-seeking is a common human behaviour. It's normal to want to be wanted. It's normal to need to be needed.

But approval-seeking behaviour can become a problem when it interferes in your personal life or your work, when you constantly seek approval from others to validate yourself or to feel good about yourself.

> Q: Are you aware of any approval-seeking behaviour
> on your behalf that happens often? If so, where
> and when does this tend to occur? What does
> this approval-seeking behaviour entail?

There are many reasons why people seek approval, but its origins can often be sourced to two main causes: fear and need.

Some common reasons for approval-seeking behaviour include:

-> Fear of looking foolish.

-> Fear of offering opinions/feelings/beliefs.

-> Fear of saying 'No'.

-> Fear of hurting another's feelings.

-> Need to belong/be accepted (fear of rejection).

Q: Consider the list of approval-seeking causes above. Do any of these resonate with you? What has been the cause of your own approval-seeking behaviour in the past?

The Need for Approval Seeking

But what is it that we are actually seeking when we seek the approval of others? What is it we are really looking for?

The answer is usually a mix of emotional, mental, and social factors, some of which include:

1. Our social nature.
2. Validation and belonging.
3. Cultural and societal norms.
4. Social learning.
5. Self-belief and confidence.
6. Comparison and competition.
7. Emotional security.

#1: Our Social Nature

Humans are inherently social creatures. We naturally gravitate to live and participate in groups and rely on the support and approval of our social networks. Seeking approval from others is a way to ensure we remain in good standing with the world.

#2: Validation and Belonging

One of our primal human needs is to belong and to be accepted. Approval from others often provides this sense of validation and belonging. It reassures us that we are accepted and valued by those around us, that we are loved. This can be a fundamental source of emotional well-being.

#3: Cultural and Societal Norms

Many cultures and societies place a strong emphasis on conformity and fitting in. Individuals may seek approval from others to adhere to these social norms and avoid ostracism or criticism. For many, what others think of us is very important.

#4: Social Learning

We learn from what we do well and from what we don't do well. External approval (or disapproval) provides feedback on our actions and behaviour, which we use to gauge our performance, make corrections, and adapt to our social environment.

#5: Self-Belief and Confidence

For some, external approval can boost our self-belief and confidence, especially children. Positive feedback from others can reinforce our sense of self-worth and encourage us to continue our efforts.

#6: Comparison and Competition

In competitive environments, we may seek external approval to assess our standing in relation to others. This can drive us to perform better or strive for excellence.

#7: Emotional Security

Receiving approval and praise from others can provide a sense of emotional security. It reduces feelings of vulnerability and inadequacy, promoting a sense of well-being.

Consequences of Low Self-Approval

Unfortunately, constant approval-seeking behaviour can get in the way of reaching your personal or professional goals, or cause you to be less effective.

The problem with an over-reliance on external validation is that only you can fill the void of low self-approval, nothing external can. Any sense that it does is fleeting and short-lived, soon leaving you with that hollow sense of despair.

As adults, constantly seeking approval from others can therefore have its downsides:

1. Dependence.
2. Anxiety and stress.
3. Inauthenticity.
4. Inhibition of creativity.
5. Lower self-approval.
6. Lost identity.

#1: Dependence

Over-reliance on external approval can lead to emotional dependence on others for your own self-identity and self-worth. This can make you highly sensitive to criticism and unable to navigate adversity.

#2: Anxiety and Stress

The constant need for approval can lead to a heightened sense of anxiety and stress. The fear of disapproval or criticism can be emotionally debilitating and mentally taxing.

#3: Inauthenticity

In your quest for external approval, you run the risk of compromising your authenticity. If you adapt your behaviour and beliefs to match what you believe others want from you, your relationships will become superficial and fragile, and you will feel a deepening sense of emptiness.

#4: Inhibition of Creativity

Constant approval seeking can hinder your creativity and prevent risk-taking. You may start to dismiss innovative or unconventional ideas or avoid taking action on these ideas for fear of disapproval or rejection.

#5: Lower Self-Approval

Paradoxically, constant approval-seeking behaviour can undermine your own self-approval and self-worth. Over time, dependence on external validation and other's opinions may cause you to question your intrinsic worth, identity, and abilities.

#6: Lost Identity

The more you seek approval from others, the further you will drift from your true self. Once your identity becomes entangled with external approval, your own values and beliefs become obscured and suppressed. You feel as though you don't know who you are anymore.

> Q: What are some consequences that approval seeking has had that stopped you from being effective in your 7 Life Segments?
> -> Family & Relationships?
> -> Career & Work?
> -> Money & Finances?
> -> Health & Wellbeing?
> -> Learning & Education?
> -> Fun & Adventure?
> -> Spirituality & Ethics?

The Benefits of Self-Approval

While external approval is important and can contribute positively to your life, it should be balanced with a strong sense of self-approval.

Achieving a healthy equilibrium between seeking external validation and fostering self-approval is essential for your overall well-being and personal growth. It allows you to maintain your authenticity, navigate challenges, and build positive, meaningful relationships.

Here are some of the benefits of prioritising self-approval:

1. Independent validation.
2. Unwavering self-belief.
3. Resilience.
4. Positive self-identity.
5. Authenticity.
6. Empowerment.
7. Positive relationships.

#1: Independent Validation

Self-approval is an internal anchor that allows you to validate yourself without the need of anything external to you. It means acknowledging your inner worth and significance without constantly seeking external approval or validation from other people or other things.

Self-approval liberates you from the ever-changing opinions and judgements of those around you, giving you a resolute sense of self-determination and complete control over your self-worth and identity.

#2: Unwavering Self-Belief

A core aspect of self-approval is the unwavering belief and inner conviction that you are deserving of love, respect, and success.

With a strong sense of self-approval, you also have belief and trust in your own judgement and abilities, irrespective of external influences or challenges.

#3: Resilience

Those who prioritise self-approval are more resilient in the face of adversity than those who seek external approval. Criticism and setbacks can be absorbed without severely damaging your self-belief and confidence.

Self-approval also bolsters your capability and capacity to bounce back from life's challenges, helping you maintain your effectiveness even in trying times.

#4: Positive Self-Identity

Self-approval forms the core of a positive self-identity, an internal source of healthy self-regard that transcends superficial markers of success, such as social status, wealth, possessions.

A positive and healthy self-identity empowers you to embrace challenges, make choices aligned with your values, and maintain a balanced and authentic self-image.

#5: Authenticity

Self-approval is intertwined with authenticity. It's the confidence to be true to yourself, embracing your wonderful uniqueness and all your imperfections.

With self-approval, you don't feel the need to conform or to mould yourself into someone you're not to gain approval from others.

#6: Empowerment

Self-approval is inherently empowering. It gives you the courage to pursue your goals, dreams, and aspirations, even in the face of criticism or doubt from external sources. Self-approval fuels the confidence to venture into the unknown and take risks.

#7: Positive Relationships

With healthy self-approval, you lay the foundation for positive, healthy relationships. When you accept and love yourself for who you are, you become more capable of forming genuine connections with others. Your relationships thrive because they become grounded in mutual respect and authenticity.

Strategies for Self-Approval

With these benefits in mind, we will now discuss four strategies to prioritise self-approval:

1. Identify approval-seeking behaviour.
2. Identify opportunities for self-approval.
3. Identify your strengths.
4. Identify your credibility.

#1: Identify Approval-Seeking Behaviour

Identifying approval-seeking behaviour is the first step towards prioritising self-approval.

When you begin to understand that your actions and decisions are frequently influenced by a deeply ingrained desire for external validation, you begin to see how much of your life is being navigated on autopilot.

You also begin to understand why you gravitate toward certain choices, relationships, or paths. In doing so, you stop being a mere bystander in your own life and begin to be an active participant in shaping your own destiny.

> Q: What approval-seeking behaviour gets in the way of you reaching your professional or personal goals or being effective?
>
> > -> What fears fuel this behaviour (see *Approval-Seeking Behaviour*)?
> >
> > -> What needs propel you to seek approval (see *The Need for Approval Seeking*)?
> >
> > -> Other?

#2: Identify Opportunities for Self-Approval

While the act of recognising your approval-seeking behaviour propels you toward empowerment, it also signifies a decisive step in reclaiming your autonomy and authenticity.

By acknowledging the fear of rejection or criticism that often underpins approval-seeking, you set the stage for personal and professional opportunities for growth. You become more effective.

> *Understanding the reasons for approval-seeking behaviour gives you the opportunity to make choices that are rooted in your values and aspirations, rather than being driven by external pressures.*

If you have identified or recognised regular approval-seeking behaviours, then the next thing to be mindful of is how to identify opportunities to prioritise self-approval over and above the need for the approval of others.

For instance, if you seek approval because you have a fear of looking foolish, how will you address this fear and give yourself approval over and above the need to receive approval from others?

As with any need, whether it's the need for food, drugs, alcohol, money, relationships, or even approval, you risk turning anything that gratifies or fulfills that need into an addiction if you do not address the underlying cause of that need.

You will simply seek more and more gratification or fulfilment of that need if the cause of that need remains untreated. Even the approval of others can become an addiction if left alone.

In my book, *Being YOU!,*[14] I discuss in detail The Cycle of Addiction and how to break the cycle. The Cycle of Addiction is a cycle of need, seeking behaviour, need fulfilment, diminished gratification, and finally more of the same need again, which triggers the whole Cycle of Addiction once more.

Figure 9 is a visual representation of the Cycle of Addiction and how it reinforces itself through constant need and gratification.

---

[14] Scott Zarcinas M.D., *Being YOU!: Awaken to the Abundance of Your Natural State of Being*, DoctorZed Publishing, 2023

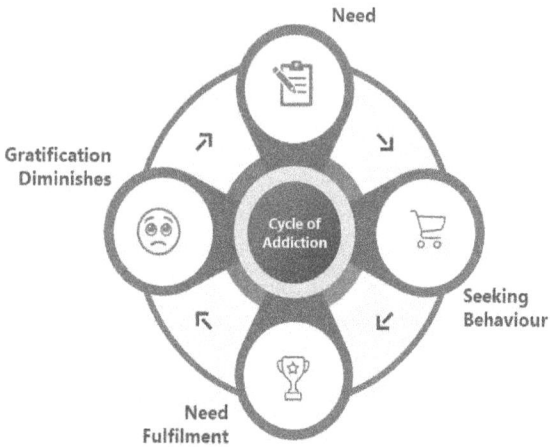

FIGURE 9:   The Cycle of Addiction

The need for approval is one such need that can trigger The Cycle of Addiction.

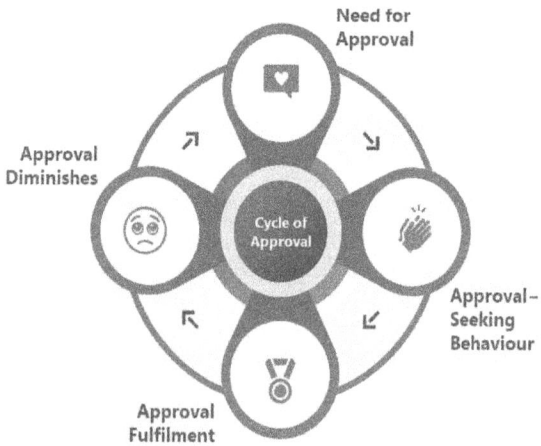

FIGURE 10:   The Cycle of Approval

The need for approval causes you to seek solutions to fulfill that need, and so you enact approval-seeking behaviour.

Even if the first person you approach doesn't give you the approval you are looking for, you'll search for someone who will. Eventually, you will find your mark and your need for approval will be fulfilled. They will give you the pat on the back you crave. Appraisal has been won. Victory is yours.

But the feeling of approval doesn't last long. Soon the appraisal diminishes and the need for approval resurfaces, triggering more approval-seeking behaviour.

Problems arise when you feel you need more and more approval from others to satisfy the need for appraisal and recognition. So much so that it becomes your dominating thought: how do you get more of what you need?

At this point, your need for approval has become an addiction. You simply can't live without it.

The best way to crush this need for another's approval and break the cycle of addiction is to root out the underlying cause. Which, more often than not, is usually a fear of some description.

For instance, if you have an underlying fear of rejection or abandonment, this can manifest as a need to be always right or perfect. If you are always right or always perfect, how can anyone reject you?

The idea of being perfect, therefore, is not a positive self-image.

It is a symptom of an underlying negative self-image, a self-image that is needy.

Being needy, you instigate approval-seeking behaviour to satisfy that need. You always insist on being right when in social settings. You demand attention. You go regularly to the gym or undergo plastic surgery to have a perfect body.

You study for years to become a doctor or lawyer or teacher, not so you can be of value to your patients or clients or students, but in order to get the social standing those job titles endow.

There are numerous ways we seek approval. We've all done it.

No-one is immune to wanting to be liked and accepted. The problem, as we've discussed, is when our need becomes an addiction. We must be aware of our fears, our needs, and our behaviours. We must be the one in control.

Otherwise, if we are not, our fears, needs, and behaviours will dominate our every waking moment.

We must therefore be alert to our underlying fears and needs driving our approval-seeking behaviour and seek out opportunities to neutralise these needs and fears through better decision-making based on our own internal values and principles. That is, you must become purpose driven.

Every choice based on your own values elevates you. Every decision founded on your own principles lifts you higher. As you free yourself from the clutches of need and fear, you free yourself from approval-seeking. As you become more self-determined, your self-identity and confidence undergo a remarkable transformation:

You start to become the architect of your own destiny, designing your life with greater intention and resolve.

With your newfound self-assuredness shining through, you are equipped with the resilience to face criticism, disapproval, or rejection with grace and courage.

From now on, your self-worth isn't contingent on external approval anymore. You start to see every moment as an opportunity to make decisions based on merit and necessity rather than the needy desire for validation.

You then start to approach your life with clarity, confidence, and strategic vision, pursuing opportunities that align with who you truly are and what you want to become.

Q: Consider the underlying fear(s) and need(s) of your approval-seeking behaviour. What are some opportunities you can identify for self-approval in your 7 Life Segments?

-> Family & Relationships?

-> Career & Work?

-> Money & Finances?

-> Health & Wellbeing?

-> Learning & Education?

-> Fun & Adventure?

-> Spirituality & Ethics?

#3: Identify Your Strengths

Now that you have identified opportunities for self-approval, the next step is to solidify the process by focusing on your strengths.

Your strengths are the unique qualities and talents that define you. They are the pillars of your identity, the attributes of character that set you apart from others. By focusing on your strengths, you acknowledge the unique value you bring to the world.

When you recognise and celebrate your strengths, whether they lie in creativity, problem-solving, empathy, leadership, or any other area, you honour the richness of your character and your capacity to make a positive impact.

Strength-based thinking also builds confidence and self-worth. This confidence is not rooted in arrogance but in a deep-seated belief in your capabilities. It empowers you to tackle challenges with optimism, knowing that your strengths will get you through times of adversity.

> *Focusing on your strengths reshapes your self-image by shifting the narrative from self-criticism and doubt to self-appreciation.*

"Focus on what you're good at doing," I often advise my children and my clients, "not on what you're not good at doing."

Too many times we trip ourselves over by focusing on the things we're not good at. When we get caught up in our own incompetence, it's as though we tie our shoelaces together and then try to run. More often than not, we fall flat on our face.

All roads may lead to Rome, but you can only travel on one. Sooner or later, you will need to make a choice. So choose the road that gives you the greatest chance of succeeding—the road of your greatest strengths.

Focus, then, on making your strengths stronger, not in making your weaknesses a little bit better.

> *When it comes to being more effective, it is better to be exceptional at one thing rather than average at a lot of things.*

That doesn't mean you shouldn't try to improve your all-round game, it means you shouldn't sacrifice your greatest strength in order to cover all your bases.

A baseball coach doesn't pressure his best pitcher to be the best hitter. He lets his pitcher do what he does best, which is pitch.

A soccer coach doesn't ask her best goalkeeper to be the best striker. She lets her goalkeeper do what she does best, which is defend the goal.

Imagine how the pitcher would feel about himself if he were asked to take the responsibility of hitting most of the runs.

Imagine how the goalkeeper would feel about herself if she were asked to take responsibility of scoring most of the goals.

It wouldn't be fair on either of them. Yet this is what we do to ourselves when we focus on our weaknesses instead of our strengths. Our performances don't meet our expectations, and we suffer for it.

We become ineffective and unproductive. We let ourselves down and we let our family and colleagues down. This has a negative impact on our self-image, which in turn has a negative impact on our performance at home and at work.

This is because the focus of your awareness is very powerful:

> *What you focus on, you experience.*

Focus on your weaknesses, and that will be your experience. Focus on your strengths, and that will be your experience. The choice is yours.

What you focus on, you also remember. Do you want to remember your weaknesses or remember your strengths?

What you focus on, you also reinforce. Do you want to reinforce your weaknesses or reinforce your strengths?

Consistent focus on your strengths, not your weaknesses, helps you to develop a healthier self-concept. This positive self-image in turn paves the way for greater emotional well-being and a more authentic relationship with yourself and others.

Yet, focusing on your strengths doesn't mean that your weaknesses are disregarded. Rather, it equips you with the maturity to address them constructively.

Identifying your strengths will give you the motivation to work on areas in need of improvement. Rather than dwelling on your shortcomings, you approach them as opportunities for growth and development.

So, focusing on your strengths will enhance your effectiveness in all aspects of your life. Whether in your career, relationships, or personal pursuits, leveraging your strengths can lead to improved performance, successful attainment of your goals, and overall confidence and well-being.

Here is an exercise that I call, 'The Strength in Me', which will help you to focus on your strengths in the most important areas of your life. Your strengths can include your talents, character traits, values, emotional intelligence, IQ, even your physical capabilities.

Some examples of people's strengths include kindness, patience, hand-eye coordination, painting, storytelling, honesty, loyalty, calmness, good work ethic, and so forth. The list is endless.

> Q: List your biggest strength in each of your 7 Life Segments:
> -> Family & Relationships
> -> Career & Work
> -> Money & Finances
> -> Health & Wellbeing
> -> Learning & Education
> -> Fun & Adventure
> -> Spirituality & Ethics

Q: Now rank your strengths in each of your 7 Life Segments in order of *biggest strength* (1-7) and give your reasons for each ranking:

1.   5.

2.   6.

3.   7.

4.

The next step in this exercise is as important to a baseball pitcher and soccer goalkeeper as it is to the development and strengthening of your innate strengths—practice.

A baseballer has practised thousands of different types of pitches before he has even strode out to the mound and struck out his first batter.

A goalkeeper has made thousands of saves before she has positioned herself between the goal posts on game day and blocked her first shot.

The same is true for your strengths. You must practice to hone your strengths so that you can perform to your highest ability and be as effective as possible as and when the situation arises.

For instance, if one of the strengths you have listed is generosity, how will you practice being generous? Will you always be generous in every given moment, or only some of the time?

Will there be conditions on your generosity? For example, will you only be generous to those in your family or who you like?

If kindness is one of the strengths you have listed, how will you practice being kind?

Will you be kind to others but not to yourself? Will you only be kind when you feel like it? Will you only be kind to those you love and ignore kindness to strangers?

> Q: Write down how you plan to hone your strengths in each of your 7 Life Segments over the next 21 days:
>
> 1.   5.
>
> 2.   6.
>
> 3.   7.
>
> 4.

#4: Identify Your Credibility

You have now identified approval-seeking behaviour, sought opportunities to give yourself self-approval first, and focused on your strengths. The final step in prioritising self-approval is to 'sell yourself to yourself'. That is, identify and accept your innate credibility.

There is an unwritten rule that you have to have credibility in business before customers will give you their money. Business coaches will tell you that if a client likes you, they'll listen to you, but if they trust you they'll do business with you.

A lack of credibility has the opposite effect, which is why businesses spend a fortune on advertising and marketing, and why they also invest in training their staff, so that customers and clients can get to know them, like them, and trust them.

The same is true in any relationship, business or social. People with high credibility have strong, trusting, meaningful relationships. Those with low credibility have fleeting, untrustworthy, and meaningless relationships.

Think of credibility as your personal 'credit rating'. In finances, when you have a high credit rating, banks and other lending institutions consider you a low risk of default on your repayments and are more likely to lend you money.

On the contrary, if you have a low credit rating, you are considered a higher risk of default on your repayments and so banks and lending institutions are less likely to lend you money. Or if they do, at a higher interest rate.

Your personal credibility is linked to your personal 'credit rating'. When others see you as credible, they lend you credit. Not necessarily in monetary or financial terms, but in relationship terms. They want to be with you. They want to do things with you. They want to spend time with you.

Because that's the most valuable thing anyone can do, give you their time. If you're not credible in another's eyes, you will not be 'worth their time'.

So the question is:

Are you worth your time?

Do you have enough internal credibility to lend more time to yourself? Do you have enough 'personal credit' to pay more attention to who you are and what you want to become?

In other words, are you credible in your own eyes?

One way to boost your internal credibility and improve your 'personal credit' is to borrow the credibility formula from the world of business, which goes like this:

$$K + L + T = C$$

K is 'know', L is 'like', T is 'trust', and C is 'credibility'.

This is how businesses raise their credibility in the marketplace. They advertise so that customers know who they are and what they sell. They focus on excellence of service and quality of product. They build trust by offering services and products that are reliable, timely, and fairly priced.

Putting all three together—know, like, trust—and credibility is the result. Credibility is just good business.

Likewise, when you put all three of these factors together, your credibility is raised in the eyes of others. When people know, like, and trust you, your personal credit rating is boosted. It's just good business.

Even better, your self-approval skyrockets when you know, like, and trust yourself. Because when you give yourself credibility, you tap into an endless credit of joy, confidence, and well-being.

Let's now discuss these three essential factors of personal credibility:

1. Know Thyself.
2. Like Thyself.
3. Trust Thyself.

K: Know Thyself

The Ancient Greeks emphasised the importance of 'knowing thyself'. In fact, so great was this belief in self-knowledge that Socrates, the father of Greek philosophy, famously opined:

The unexamined life is not worth living.

Self-knowledge is the core of personal growth and self-development. Growth and development—evolution—is life's essential nature, which in a nutshell is 'change'.

When you grow and develop—evolve—you are aligned with, and in harmony with, your natural state, which is change.

Self-knowledge is the catalyst for personal evolution.

Personal evolution is personal transformation. It's becoming that which you intend to be.

But for that to happen you must embrace your true nature and deliberately and intentionally grow, expand, change. You must evolve.

You must embrace who you are, not deny who you are. You must be like water and 'go with the flow', not resist who you are and become stationary. You must know yourself, not ignore yourself.

But without deliberate examination of yourself and the understanding that comes with it, your growth will naturally be stunted and your development limited—you will not evolve.

Those who do not evolve remain the same, which is ultimately to become stagnant and resistant to the natural flow of life.

This has obvious repercussions to your personal success and effectiveness, not to mention the detrimental effects on your physical, mental, emotional, and spiritual well-being:

> *That which stagnates invariably ages, decays, and dies before its time.*

To 'know thyself' then is to live a life of fullness, to live a life worth living.

So far in this chapter on prioritising self-approval, we've looked at several aspects of yourself in which you can get to 'know thyself' better, such as:

- Your awareness.
- Your behaviours.
- Your fears and needs.
- Your strengths.

These are just some of the aspects of yourself you can begin to investigate and get to know, get to 'realise', who you really are—the self behind your thoughts, emotions, and behaviours.

For that's precisely what 'knowing thyself' is, self-realisation— the realisation of your true self, the self that has hitherto been hidden and unknown and is now being made aware and known.

Some other aspects of yourself you can investigate and bring to your awareness include:

- Your higher intelligence.
- Your 'I am'.
- Your beliefs.
- Your unconditional love.
- Your limitless and eternal soul.

The emphasis on 'knowing thyself' is on who you are, not what you do. On who you are *being* while you do what you are doing.

For instance, as we discussed in *Chapter 2: Clarity & Purpose*, in the Life Segment *Family & Relationships*, you have many roles in which you are a son/daughter, mother/father, brother/ sister, cousin, friend, mentor, husband/wife/partner, aunty/ uncle, grandmother/grandfather, and so forth.

But these relationship roles are what you do within the context of family, they are not the 'who' behind what you do. They are only a label describing your current experience, not the 'you' that is experiencing this current role.

As we mentioned before, you can't do without being, but you can be without doing. As such, our labels are self-limiting—they limit the definition of who you are to a designation.

But you are more than a designation. Your labels change when circumstances change, so they are only temporary and therefore cannot define who you really are, because you are not temporary.

> *You are the permanent experiencer of all your experiences.*

When you were a child you had a label of son or daughter, sister or brother. You were not labelled as a mother or father, wife or husband. Those labels came later in life, added on to your definition of you and what you now do.

But the 'you' experiencing these new labels didn't change. The essence of who you are remained the same and still remains the same, no matter what new labels you pin to your chest.

In the sub-chapter *Being & Doing: The 7 Life Segments*, I asked you to consider who you are *being* in each role of your 7 Life Segments. Because when you focus on who you are being, you will notice that you are the same 'you' in each and every role that you play in life.

> *Your 'you' is permanent. Your 'you' doesn't change. Only your labels change.*

Let's use my current roles as an example:

-> Family & Relationships: son, brother, grandson, father, husband, cousin, friend.

-> Career & Work: transformational coach, writer, publisher, author, speaker, mentor, volunteer, workshop presenter, business owner, entrepreneur, employer.

-> Money & Finances: wage earner, investor, budget keeper, homeowner, car owner, 'Daddy bank'.

-> Health & Wellbeing: 50's, regular gym attendee, no major health issues, omnivore, non-smoker.

-> Learning & Education: university-educated, post-graduate certificates, digital marketing, business development, editing and proofreading.

-> Fun & Adventure: traveller, golfer, cricket lover, football fan, beachgoer.

-> Spirituality & Ethics: meditator, spiritual pilgrim, Christian, truth seeker, lover of life.

These are just some of the many labels I pin to my chest, but they are not 'me' per se. These labels keep changing as I pass through various life stages. They are just what I am currently experiencing in *my conscious reality* at this moment.

I haven't always been a father or a husband or a writer. I was once a school student, and later a medical student at university, and then a doctor. That was then, but this is now, and in the future I hope to wear the label of grandfather and international speaker and bestselling author.

But no matter which label I wear in the past, present, or future, I am still the same 'me'. I am that which is aware of the roles I play and the labels I wear. I am that which is conscious of the conditions in which I am living out this life here on Earth.

I am aware of my thoughts. I am aware of my emotions. I am aware of my body. I am aware of the people, places, things, and events happening 'outside' of me.

And I am aware of my awareness of these things.

Awareness is who I am. It's who you are too. You are in this world but not of it. You are consciousness itself.

> *There are no limits to your awareness, the only limits are that which you choose to be aware of. The only limits are the conditions upon which you choose to focus.*

When you focus your awareness on things—thoughts, emotions, impulses, beliefs, conditions, events, time—you infuse your sense of self into that thing's form and it becomes your experience.

But when you focus on your unlimited awareness, that too will be your experience—limitless *being*.

The focus of your attention, therefore, is the means by which you stop being a flea in the flea circus and start living a life of fulfilled potential. It's how you go beyond your limits.

It's how you get to truly know thyself.

L: Like Thyself

The next part of the credibility equation is to like yourself.

Do you like yourself? Do you like who you've become? If you could somehow go to a party and meet yourself for the first time, would you like this person you've just met?

Frances Scovel Shinn, author of the bestselling book, *The Game of Life and How to Play It*, said this about the importance of liking yourself in a compilation of her works, *The Power of the Spoken Word: Teachings of Frances Scovel Shinn*:[15]

> *The first start toward success is to be glad you are yourself. So many people are bored by themselves. They have no self-reliance, and they are always wishing they were somebody else.*

So many people trip themselves up on the road to success because they don't like who they are. They are not glad they are themselves. They are not happy in their own skin.

We all know or have heard of so-called successful millionaires who are miserly and miserable. Despite their outward success, they are deeply unhappy.

No matter how many houses and cars they own, no matter how much money they have, no matter how much others think they are 'worth', they still feel incomplete and of little or no inner value.

---

[15] Frances Scovel Shinn, *The Power of the Spoken Word: Teachings of Frances Scovel Shinn*, Shinn Press, 1944

This is because they are trying to do the impossible—they are trying to create inside what they have created on the outside.

This is the real 'mission impossible' they have tasked themselves, to achieve happiness through external possession. They are trying to be happy through 'getting stuff' or 'doing stuff'. The more stuff they get or do, they reason, the more they'll be happy.

They are trying to control their inner world and sense of worth through the control of external conditions and events.

This they keep striving to achieve for years, even decades. Even a whole lifetime. But it's all to no avail because no-one and no-thing can make you feel happy about yourself, only you can.

Only you can reveal yourself to yourself. External events, people, places, things, money, can certainly act as a mirror to reflect what's going on inside you. But you can't experience yourself through a reflection in a mirror. The reflection is not you. The image, any image, is not you. It can't be.

You are that which experiences the reflection, and to lose your sense of self in the mirror is to forget who it is that is creating the reflection.

It is to forget who you truly are. It is to forget your natural state of joy, peace, and freedom—to forget your abundant self.

There are, of course, happy millionaires, but they aren't happy because of the value of their assets, they are happy because they are happy with who they are.

They know they are not the reflection in the mirror. They know their money and possessions do not define them. They know that circumstances and conditions do not make them who they are, but instead *reveal* who they are.

Success and happiness, contrary to what society will tell you, has more to do with who you are being than what you have or what you are doing. Abundance is internal, not external.

The experience of abundance is simply an expression of being happy and feeling successful irrespective of your external conditions and circumstances.

Any material abundance—money, possessions, social status, positions of power—that you may attain are secondary to how glad you are being yourself, of how rich your life feels internally.

> *Successful people aren't happy because of what they have, they are happy because of who they are.*

Therefore, in order to like yourself more, to be glad you are yourself and to give yourself the best start toward success, you must endeavour to know thyself and to become your best friend.

You must treat yourself exactly as you would treat your best friend, with kindness, compassion, understanding, forgiveness, humour, assistance, non-judgement, generosity, love.

> Q: Consider your 7 Life Segments. How will you focus on liking yourself more in each segment?

T: Trust Thyself

Now that you have gotten to know yourself better and to like yourself more, the remaining part of the credibility equation is to trust yourself.

For many people, however, distrust is more often the norm. Not just the distrust of others, but the distrust of themselves.

In fact, the underlying reason why people distrust others is because they actually don't trust themselves. They project their own misgivings about themselves onto others. They think everyone else is just like them, untrustworthy.

When we find it hard to trust ourselves, it's only natural that extending trust to others is an even greater hurdle. The seeds of doubt we sow within ourselves tend to grow into weeds of mistrust when dealing with external relationships.

But if you can't rely on your own judgement, how can you possibly trust the judgements of those around you?

If you can't trust yourself, how on Earth are you going to trust somebody else?

You can't.

> Q: What can you do to trust yourself more and boost your 'personal credit' and self-credibility in each of your 7 Life Segments?

Main Points:

1. Self-approval is an essential component of personal well-being. It signifies the capacity to trust your own judgements, decisions, and actions, free from the relentless need for external validation.
2. Achieving a healthy equilibrium between seeking external validation and fostering self-approval is essential for your overall well-being and personal growth.
3. There are many reasons why people seek approval, but its origins can often be sourced to two main causes: fear and need.
4. Identifying approval-seeking behaviour is the first step towards prioritising self-approval.
5. Understanding the reasons for approval-seeking behaviour gives you the opportunity to make choices that are rooted in your values and aspirations, rather than being driven by external pressures.
6. Focusing on your strengths reshapes your self-image by shifting the narrative from self-criticism and doubt to self-appreciation.
7. What you focus on, you experience.
8. When you give yourself credibility, you tap into an endless credit of joy, confidence, and well-being.
9. Self-knowledge is the catalyst for personal evolution.
10. The first start toward success is to be glad you are yourself.
11. Successful people aren't happy because of what they have, they are happy because of who they are.

10 BETTER THAN PERFECT

'Don't let the perfect be the enemy of the good.'
Volataire

STRIVING FOR PERFECTION can instill within you an unrelenting drive to excel. At one end, the pursuit of perfection encourages you to exceed your personal horizons. But at the other end, it carries a burden of frustration, disappointment, fatigue, and stress.

The perfectionist, feeling far from her goals, resorts to working harder, sleeping less, and sacrificing the balance between her work and life.

For when you demand perfection from yourself, you pursue an ideal that is forever elusive, forever beyond your grasp.

> *Perfectionism presents as unrealistically high standards accompanied by the tendency to be overly critical in the evaluation of yourself or others.*

Perfectionism affects all areas of our life: career, academia, parenthood, physical appearance, relationships. But this unrelenting drive often conceals a deeper longing—a yearning to be liked, accepted, and valued.

Psychologists recognise that perfectionism has complex roots. They see perfectionism as a tapestry woven from the threads of personality, childhood experiences, demanding expectations, and the ceaseless clamour of perfection blasting from society and the media.

Here are some questions you might like to consider to see if you have any perfectionistic habits or tendencies that you might want to work on:

- Do you set exceptionally high standards for yourself, and also for others?

- Do you downplay your achievements and feel inadequate despite your achievements?

- Do you delay or ignore certain tasks out of fear you might not do them perfectly?

- Do you engage in self-criticism or negative self-talk for any flaws, faults, or mistakes?

- Do you frequently dwell on what you 'could' or 'should' have done differently?

If you've answered 'yes' to one or more of these questions, chances are you might have a perfectionistic streak.

Consequences of Perfectionism

Although not always negative, perfectionism can exert a powerful influence on all aspects of your life with far-reaching consequences.

Yet, while there's nothing wrong with hard work and high

standards, the irony is that perfectionism can undermine your effectiveness.

There is a vast bank of research that underscores the problems of perfectionism, which can overwhelm your life if you do nothing about it, so we will now discuss some examples of the negative effects that perfectionism can have on your:

1. Mental health.
2. Relationships.
3. Career and work.
4. Attainment of goals.

#1: Mental Health

The relentless pursuit of perfection, combined with the fear of failure, can create a cocktail of emotional distress.

Perfectionists tend to set impossibly high standards for themselves, leading to chronic dissatisfaction and constant self-criticism.

For instance, studies have shown a strong link between perfectionism and mental health issues,[16] in particular elevated levels of stress, anxiety, and depression.

Perfectionism has also been linked to rumination, a repetitive focus on your mistakes and shortcomings, which can intensify symptoms of anxiety and depression.

---

[16] Paul Hewitt and Gordon Flett, Perfectionism in the self and social contexts, *Journal of Personality and Social Psychology*, 1991

#2: Relationships

Because perfectionists can struggle with the challenges and complexities of interpersonal dynamics, both socially and professionally, perfectionism can significantly impact personal relationships.[17]

The relentless pursuit of perfection can lead to unrealistic expectations of yourself and others, resulting in strained relationships.

Partners, friends, and family members may feel inadequate or fear being constantly criticised, which can erode trust and prevent intimacy.

The fear of rejection or abandonment because you believe 'you're not perfect or good enough' can also make you overly cautious in forming new relationships.

Which means your perfectionism can result in social isolation and loneliness if you allow it to go unchecked.

#3: Career

While perfectionism may drive individuals to achieve high levels of success, it can also hinder your career progression through impaired job performance and job-related stress, what's known as maladaptive perfectionism.

This is because perfectionists often engage in procrastination, have a fear of taking risks, and excessively ruminate about work.

---

[17] Paul Hewitt et. al., Perfection and interpersonal problems, *Journal of Personality and Social Psychology,* 2006: Vol 90

The pursuit of unattainable standards can also prevent collaboration with others and sabotage teamwork, further isolating you and hindering your productivity and efficiency.

#4: Attainment of Goals

Researchers have also revealed a negative association between perfectionism and goal attainment.[18]

This happens when the relentless pursuit of perfection leads to procrastination as you wait for the 'perfect' conditions to act.

When you feel that everything has to be perfect in order for you to do your work, you risk missing the opportunities that present to you whilst at the same time delaying the achievement of personal and professional goals.

To paraphrase Winston Churchill:

Perfectionism spells paralysis.

Strategies for 'Letting Go, and Letting Good'

While perfectionism is sometimes viewed as a trait that drives success, there is no doubt about its damaging consequences for your mental health, relationships, career, and goal attainment.

It is therefore essential to understand the nuanced nature of perfectionism and to strive for a healthier balance, where the pursuit of perfection does not come at the cost of well-being, relationships, and your effectiveness.

---

[18] Gordon Flett and Paul Hewitt, *Perfectionism: Theory, Research, and Treatment*, American Psychological Association, 2002

> *Not everyone who is trapped in the flea circus is a perfectionist, but every perfectionist is trapped in the flea circus.*

Recognising the signs of maladaptive perfectionism and seeking support when needed is a crucial step in nullifying its consequences and achieving a more balanced and fulfilling life.

The key to finding balance is self-reflection. You need to investigate the origins of your perfectionist tendencies and understand the adverse effects they have on your life. Then you need to stop using your productivity and achievements (what you do) as unrelenting standards with which you judge your self-worth and form your self-image (who you are).

In other words, you need to let go of the belief that you have to be perfect in order to be 'good enough', valuable, or acceptable.

You already are good enough. You already are valuable. You already are acceptable. You don't need to be perfect; in fact, it just gets in the way. It gets in the way of everything.

What you need to do is start prioritising good over perfect, what I call 'Letting Go, and Letting Good'.

Only when you let go of the need to be perfect and accept that good is good enough will you begin to unburden the heavy weight of perfectionism and enjoy the positive benefits in your mental and emotional well-being, your relationships, your career, and the achievement of your goals.

We will now discuss four strategies to prioritise good over perfect:

1. Recognise your need for perfectionism and/or your perfectionistic behaviour.

2. Be curious as to why you need to be perfect.

3. Observe the effect of your perfectionism.

4. Challenge yourself: The 90% Rule.

#1: Recognise Your Need for Perfectionism

Perfectionism is often a significant roadblock on our journey to achieving personal and professional goals.

The first step to 'Letting Go, and Letting Good' and learning how to prioritise good over perfect is recognising the various dimensions of perfectionism in all aspects of your life. This is crucial for understanding how perfectionism hinders your progress and well-being and overall effectiveness.

> Q: What perfectionistic thoughts or behaviour get in the way of you reaching your professional or personal goals or being effective?
>
> -> Unrelenting high standards?
>
> -> Self-judgement or self-worth?
>
> -> Inability to start/finish tasks?
>
> -> Are you seeking perfection or excellence?
>
> -> Need to belong/be accepted?
>
> -> Risk aversion?

#2: Be Curious

Next, be curious to the reasons why you need to be perfect. This is crucial if you truly want to be more effective.

Understanding the compulsion to be perfect will help you to develop strategies to shift from rigid perfectionism to a balanced and more flexible approach to your tasks.

Unrelenting High Standards

Is the relentless pursuit of perfection stemming from a deep-seated desire for exceptional achievement?

While high standards can be motivating, they can also evolve into an inflexible pursuit of perfection that cause frustration and demotivation when unattainable objectives are not met.

Self-Judgement and Self-Worth

Is the need for perfection driven by the tendency to be exceptionally self-critical?

Although learning from your mistakes is important and vital for your overall success, self-criticism that associates self-worth with accomplishments builds immense self-imposed pressure that dampens your personal and professional effectiveness.

Inability to Start/Finish Tasks

Is the compulsion for perfection a manifestation of an overpowering fear of initiating or completing tasks?

The perceived magnitude of the task and the fear of falling short of perfection can often lead to procrastination. This delay, in turn, hinders productivity and goal attainment.

Seeking Perfection vs. Excellence

Are you pursuing perfection or pursuing excellence?

It's vital to know the difference between the two. Perfectionism can drive you to seek an unattainable ideal, whereas aiming for excellence involves a more constructive approach to continuous self-improvement by allowing mistakes and imperfections to become integral components of your journey to success..

Need to Belong/Be Accepted

Is the quest for perfection intertwined with a need for external validation and acceptance?

This may be driven by a fear of rejection or judgement from others, leading to the belief that only perfection can guarantee your place within a group or community.

In the long term, this need for external validation can diminish your authenticity and impede your personal and professional development.

Risk Aversion

Is perfectionism manifesting as an aversion to risk-taking?

This can be due to a fear of failure or success, an obsession with order and control, or an intense dislike of criticism or disapproval.

Each of these facets can hinder your journey toward achieving personal and professional goals and impede your overall effectiveness.

Q: What do you understand about the reasons why you need to be perfect? Can you identify any of the following compulsions:

-> Desire for exceptionally high standards?

-> Self-criticism?

-> Fear of initiating or completing tasks?

-> Pursuit of perfection or excellence?

-> Need for external validation and acceptance?

-> Fear of failure or success?

#3: Observe the Effect of Your Perfectionism

The next step to 'Letting Go, and Letting Good' is to be aware of the effect that perfection has on all areas of your life.

Self-awareness is key. Acknowledging the presence of perfectionism within yourself and the effects it has is an essential component to releasing its hold over you.

So take the time to reflect on the areas of your life where you may have unrealistic expectations or an intrinsic fear of making mistakes. Recognising the pervasive nature of perfectionism and observing its effects allows you to begin the process of freeing your thoughts and actions from its influence.

Self-Improvement

Perfectionism can manifest in various forms—setting impossibly high standards, relentless self-criticism, and chronic procrastination.

By observing these dimensions, you gain insight into how they may be impeding your personal growth. It enables you to pinpoint specific areas where you need to let go of perfection and embrace a healthier approach to self-improvement.

Well-Being

Perfectionism can exact a toll on your mental and emotional well-being.

Psychologists tell us that the need to be perfect is often accompanied by heightened stress, anxiety, and a constant sense of inadequacy.

Observing the emotional strain that perfectionism imposes on your well-being underscores the urgency of adopting a more balanced perspective.

Prioritising 'good' over 'perfect' means prioritising your well-being, so use this as a driving force to let go of the relentless pursuit of perfection.

Professional Effectiveness

In your professional work, you may notice that perfectionism undermines your productivity and hinders opportunities for career development through procrastination, a fear of taking calculated risks, and substandard job performance.

By identifying the manifestations of perfectionism in your working life, you can develop a strategic plan to address these barriers and enhance your overall effectiveness and career progression.

Balanced Living

Perfectionism is not confined to one area of your life but in fact permeates every aspect of your 7 Life Segments, from personal relationships to health and well-being, to learning and education, to career and work.

Observing its impact across these areas will motivate you to create more balance and harmony in your life. Letting go of the need for perfectionism and embracing 'good' allows you to allocate your energy and time effectively, enhancing your overall quality of life.

> Q: What have been some observable effects of perfectionism in your life? Can you identify any negative effects in the following scenarios:
>
> -> Self-improvement and personal growth?
>
> -> Mental and emotional well-being?
>
> -> Career development and progression?
>
> -> Balance and harmony?

#4: Challenge Yourself: The 90% Rule

Recognising, understanding, and observing the many and varied ways perfectionism affects your life and keeps you trapped in the flea circus is vital to increasing your effectiveness and guiding you toward a more balanced and fulfilling life.

As you become more aware of the negative influence that perfectionism has upon you, you begin to take more proactive measures to lessen its effects, cultivate resilience, and prioritise 'good' over the unattainable 'perfect.'

This shift in perspective ultimately enhances your progress, well-being, and overall effectiveness in every facet of life.

One shift in perspective is to embrace the 90% Rule and to accept that 'good is good enough'.

As productivity coaches like to say:

> *Done is better than perfect.*

> *The 90% Rule states that something completed to 90% satisfaction is far better than striving for unrealistic 110% perfection.*

The 90% Rule represents a paradigm shift that can profoundly impact each and every segment of your life.

By accepting that perfection beyond a certain point is neither feasible nor beneficial, you grant yourself the freedom to be more efficient, reduce stress, promote creativity, embrace growth, maintain relationships, and advance in your career.

Efficiency and Productivity

The 90% Rule acknowledges that there comes a point where the additional effort invested in achieving perfection yields diminishing returns.

Striving for that 110% perfection (because perfectionists don't just do 100%, do they?) can be incredibly time-consuming and resource-intensive, often without a proportional improvement in the final outcome.

Embracing the 90% Rule allows you to channel your efforts more efficiently, promoting productivity and saving your most valuable resource—time.

Reduced Stress and Anxiety

Perfectionism can be a significant source of stress and anxiety because the incessant pursuit of flawless results can lead to unrelenting self-criticism and the fear of making mistakes.

By acknowledging the 90% Rule, you grant yourself the gift of reduced stress. You let go of the unrealistic demands for absolute perfection and replace these demands with a more forgiving and compassionate approach to your work and life.

Increased Innovation and Creativity

The pursuit of perfection can stifle creativity and innovation because when you're fixated on achieving an unattainable standard, you may become risk-averse and reluctant to explore new ideas.

In contrast, accepting the 90% Rule provides room for experimentation and the freedom to take creative risks. This mindset can lead to breakthroughs and novel solutions.

Enhanced Learning and Growth

Recognising that 90% satisfaction is an acceptable achievement, you become more open to learning from your experiences.

When mistakes and imperfections are viewed as valuable opportunities for growth rather than as failures, this perspective promotes resilience and adaptability, enabling you to grow personally and professionally.

Maintaining Relationships

Perfectionism can extend to interpersonal relationships, where excessively high standards and a critical attitude can strain intimacy with loved ones and weaken connections with friends and colleagues.

Embracing the 90% Rule can lead to healthier, more balanced relationships by allowing you to appreciate the imperfections in both yourself and others, which nurtures greater understanding and acceptance.

Career Advancement

The 90% Rule can also be a catalyst for career advancement. Rather than obsessing over unattainable perfection, you can focus on excellence instead, delivering consistently reliable work, and regularly meeting deadlines.

This approach can lead to greater recognition from superiors and fellow workers, and enhance your career opportunities.

Here are some everyday scenarios of the differences between striving for 110% perfection and the implementation of the 90% Rule. These examples illustrate how perfectionism can lead to delays in various aspects of you life, hindering your progress, and that aiming for 90% is a practical alternative to perfectionism.

> Assumption #1: "I won't find the perfect time to start, so I'll delay it."

-> Perfectionistic Belief: Delaying the house cleaning because you need to find the perfect moment for it to be done spotlessly.

-> 90% is Good Enough: Accept that there's no perfect time, aim to complete 90% of the cleaning now, and set realistic standards.

Assumption #2: "It has to be absolutely impeccable, so I'll do it later."

-> Perfectionistic Belief: Delay organising or decorating your home because you insist on achieving perfection, leading to inaction.

-> 90% is Good Enough: Start organising or decorating with the goal of 90% satisfaction, recognising that it doesn't have to be absolutely impeccable.

Assumption #3: "I must perfect every detail, so I'll finish it eventually."

-> Perfectionistic Belief: You procrastinate at work completing tasks because you believe you must perfect every detail, which can result in missed deadlines.

-> 90% is Good Enough: Focus on achieving 90% completion within the given time frame, allowing for minor imperfections.

Assumption #4: "I need to make the best choice, so I'll decide later."

-> Perfectionistic Belief: Delay making decisions for fear of making the wrong choice, leading to delays in both personal and professional life.

-> 90% is Good Enough: Recognise that decisions can be adjusted if needed, and aim to make choices that are 90% in line with your goals.

The principle aim of the 90% Rule is to enhance your effectiveness in navigating the complexities of modern life in a balanced way and without the stress of perfectionism.

So now you how to 'Let Go, and Let Good'. As John Steinbeck's character, Lee, tells Abra in his bestselling novel, *East of Eden*:[19]

And now that you don't have to be perfect, you can be good.

Q: What can you do now to focus on 'Letting Go, and Letting Good' and prioritise the 90% Rule in each of your 7 Life Segments?

-> Family & Relationships?

-> Career & Work?

-> Money & Finances?

-> Health & Wellbeing?

-> Learning & Education?

-> Fun & Adventure?

-> Spirituality & Ethics?

---

[19] John Steinbeck, *East of Eden*, Viking Press, 1952

MAIN POINTS:

1. Perfectionism presents as unrealistically high standards accompanied by the tendency to be overly critical in the evaluation of yourself or others.
2. While perfectionism is sometimes viewed as a trait that drives success, there is no doubt about its damaging consequences for your mental health, relationships, career, and goal attainment.
3. Not everyone who is trapped in the flea circus is a perfectionist, but every perfectionist is trapped in the flea circus.
4. Understanding the compulsion to be perfect will help you to develop strategies to shift from rigid perfectionism to a balanced and more flexible approach to your tasks.
5. Recognising the pervasive nature of perfectionism and observing its effects allows you to begin the process of freeing your thoughts and actions from its influence.
6. Done is better than perfect.
7. The 90% Rule represents a paradigm shift that can profoundly impact each and every segment of your life.

11 EFFECTIVE SELF-TALK

'Some people grumble that roses have thorns; I am
grateful that thorns have roses."

Alphonse Karr

IN THE LAST four chapters we have been discussing the first
area of need in establishing good self-management practices:
identifying self-limiting *habits* and the strategies you can
implement to overcome these habits.

In this chapter, we will focus on the second area of need of
good self-management: identifying self-limiting *thoughts* and
the strategies you can implement to overcome these thoughts.

As we've discussed, one of the fundamental tenets of this
guidebook is that your thoughts create your world. What you
focus on you experience, in other words.

> *What you give your attention to becomes your
> conscious reality.*

People get trapped in the flea circus because they believe they
are limited. They turn their world into a flea circus through
their negative thoughts and self-limiting beliefs.

The flea circus isn't something you buy a ticket for and enter
into, it's something you create. You build your own circus with
your own thoughts.

Believe it or not, you are the star of your own show, the ringmaster of your own personal circus. You get trapped in your own world of thoughts and beliefs, creating a circus of limitation, frustration, unhappiness, and futility.

But the good news is, you can escape your own creation. You can escape your personal flea circus. This you do through the only way out available to you—your consciousness.

You cannot experience anything without first being conscious of it. Without consciousness, you cannot experience anything at all. That means nothing. Not a single thing.

Consciousness is the means by which you experience life. Therefore, the answer to changing your experience from ineffectiveness to effectiveness is through your consciousness.

I remember a day in the early 90s when this realisation hit me like a cold slap. I was in my mid-20s and was walking with a friend in London through the back streets from Earls Court to South Kensington.

It was a beautiful spring day, but I barely noticed it. I was lost in negative thoughts and complaining non-stop to my friend how bad my life situation was. Women didn't like me. I couldn't find a girlfriend. I wasn't very attractive. I was running out of money. I didn't like my job. The list went on and on and on.

Suddenly, my friend stopped in his tracks. He had had enough of my constant complaining and moaning. "You know what, Scott?" he said. "You are the most negative person on the planet!"

I too stopped in my tracks. The most negative person on the *planet*! Me? How was that possible? He was joking, right?

But, no, he wasn't joking. My friend was speaking the truth, and it hurt. I was at a loss for words. I just stood there, mouth ajar, as if he had just dumped a whole cooler bin of ice on top of my head.

As painful as it was to hear, I knew in my heart that I was an extremely negative person. I did complain a lot. I did moan a lot. I did think that my life was a misery and that others had it far better than me. I did feel as though life was pretty unfair, and that I had been dealt a bad set of cards.

It was obvious that in that moment I had been brought to a crossroad. A decision had to be made. A decision that could no longer be ignored. Remain the same and continue the way things were—unhappy, miserable, frustrated, downbeat, lonely—or change and do things differently?

But I couldn't remain the same. I simply couldn't. Things needed to change for the better, and they needed to change quickly. I knew there really was no other choice.

I also knew that if I wanted my life to change, I had to change. I had to change the way I viewed the world. I had to change the way I viewed myself. I had to change the way I viewed my interaction with the world.

I knew too that only I could change the things I wanted changing. I knew that only I could change my world, and I knew that in order to do so I had to be that change myself.

I had to change my perception—my *perspective*—and the only feasible way to do that was to change where that perspective happens—the focus of my attention, my conscious awareness.

On that beautiful spring day somewhere between Earls Court and South Kensington, I made a vow to become the most *positive* person on the planet!

Negative Self-Talk

Did the metamorphosis into Mr. Positive happen overnight? Of course not.

But what did happen was my instant awareness of my own negative thought patterns, which then made me aware of my negative emotional patterns, which then made me aware of my negative speech patterns, which then made me aware of my negative behavioural patterns. It was the beginning of change.

Negative or self-limiting thoughts are extremely common, probably a lot more common than you would think. In fact, it's mind-boggling how prevalent negative thinking is.

I once made a calculation on how many negative words the average person says to himself or herself in an average year. I based it on the amount of thoughts psychologists have estimated that go through a person's mind on a daily basis, coupled with the estimate that of those thoughts, 80% are negative. The results were staggering:

> *The average person has 3-17 million negative thoughts per year.*

That's astounding. But then I multiplied that figure by the average lifetime of 80 years and arrived at this unbelievable conclusion: as a species, we humans have 240-1,360 million negative thoughts per person, per lifetime (and yes, that's 1.36 billion at the top end).

I sat back in shock. But then I considered the opposite of this and what it could mean. Just imagine, I thought, the person who has 1.36 billion *positive* thoughts in their lifetime.

Imagine what they could achieve. Imagine the power of good they could do for others and their community. Imagine the paradise they could create for the world.

Imagine if it were you.

Consequences of Negative Thinking

The problem with continuous negative thinking is the damaging influence it has in all areas of your life, from self-doubt in your professional work to guilt in accepting blame for external factors beyond your control.

The impact is magnified if negative self-talk is allowed to dominate your consciousness over the entirety of your life.

Recognising the patterns of negative thinking through self-awareness is the first step in addressing and reframing these thoughts and beliefs to promote a more positive and constructive mindset.

Here are some common ineffective or self-limiting thought processing that often run through our minds:

-> Self-Doubt: Questioning your abilities and fearing that you're not good enough.

-> Catastrophising: Expecting the worst-case scenario in every situation.

-> All-or-Nothing Thinking: Believing that if you can't do something perfectly, it's not worth doing at all.

-> Overgeneralisation: Drawing broad, negative conclusions from a single negative event.

-> Self-Criticism: Engaging in harsh self-criticism and negative internal dialogue.

-> Mind Reading: Assuming you know what others are thinking, usually assuming they are making negative judgements about you.

-> Personalisation: Taking responsibility for things outside your control or blaming yourself for events unrelated to you.

-> Should Statements: Setting rigid and unrealistic expectations for yourself and others.

-> Filtering: Focusing solely on the negative aspects of a situation and ignoring the positive.

-> Discounting the Positive (Imposter Syndrome): Minimising or dismissing your achievements and positive qualities.

The below table is a summary of some common negative self-talk that arise from ineffective thought processing.

EFFECTIVE SELF-TALK

INEFFECTIVE THINKING	NEGATIVE SELF-TALK
Self-Doubt	I'll never be able to succeed in this new job. I don't have the skills or experience.
Catastrophising	If I don't ace this presentation, my entire career will be ruined.
All-or-Nothing	If I can't commit to working out for an hour every day, there's no point in even trying to get in shape.
Overgeneralisation	I messed up that report, so I'm terrible at my job and always will be.
Self-Criticism	I'm such a failure. I can't do anything right, and I'll never be successful.
Mind Reading	I just know my coworkers are talking behind my back and criticising my work.
Personalisation	It's my fault that the project failed. I should have done more to prevent it.
Should Statements	I should be working late every night to prove my dedication to the company.
Filtering	Despite all the praise I received for my presentation, I can't stop thinking about the one person who didn't seem impressed.
Discounting the Positive (Imposter Syndrome)	Sure, I got a promotion, but it was probably just luck. I'm not really that capable.

TABLE 8: Ineffective Thinking & Negative Self-Talk

Q: What are some consequences that ineffective thinking and negative self-talk has had that stopped you from being effective in your 7 Life Segments?

-> Family & Relationships?

-> Career & Work?

-> Money & Finances?

-> Health & Wellbeing?

-> Learning & Education?

-> Fun & Adventure?

-> Spirituality & Ethics?

Strategies for Effective Thinking

I have witnessed the life-changing benefits of addressing and reframing negative and self-limiting thoughts from a personal perspective as well as witnessing the amazing transformation of clients who have embraced the process of conscious mindshift.

If you were to ask me what is the most important factor in The Effectiveness Equation, $E = MC^2$, I would answer without hesitation, "Mindset."

Of course, your capability and capacity are important factors in your personal and professional effectiveness, but mindset is critical. If you were to choose just one thing to focus on, I would advise you to focus on your mindset.

Without the right mindset, your effectiveness is near zero, no matter how capable you are or how much capacity you have.

I would go so far as to say that mindset is responsible for 80% of your effectiveness, and your capability and capacity, which we will soon discuss in *Part 3*, are responsible for the remaining 20% of your effectiveness.

Which is why we have spent so much time on getting your mindset right. Your mindset is the Swiss army knife of personal growth and emotional well-being, the very tool you need to carry everywhere you go to navigate challenges, build resilience, and approach life with a more positive and constructive outlook. That is, to be effective.

Having the right mindset empowers you in various ways:

Resilience and Adaptability

A positive and constructive mindset bolsters your resilience in the face of challenges. Instead of succumbing to negative thought patterns, you develop the ability to adapt and bounce back from setbacks.

You view obstacles as opportunities for growth and learning, enhancing your overall capacity to navigate life's ups and downs.

Focus on Strengths

The right mindset encourages you to focus on your strengths rather than dwelling on your perceived weaknesses. It leads to a greater awareness and realistic assessment of your skillset and capabilities.

By acknowledging and capitalising on your strengths, you amplify your personal and professional effectiveness.

Healthier Relationships

Cultivating the right mindset promotes healthier relationships. When you no longer engage in self-limiting thought patterns, you can approach interactions with authenticity and emotional intelligence.

This promotes more meaningful and positive connections with others, improving your personal and professional relationships.

Greater Confidence

A positive and constructive mindset instills confidence. You're more willing to take calculated risks and pursue opportunities, knowing that setbacks are part of the journey to success.

This newfound confidence empowers you to excel in your professional life and take on personal challenges with optimism and enthusiasm.

We will now discuss four strategies to help develop the right mindset by prioritising effective thinking over ineffective thinking:

1. Identify Ineffective Thinking.
2. The STOP Method.
3. Effective Self-Talk.
4. Effective Value.

#1: Identify Ineffective Thinking

Identifying ineffective thinking is the first step in prioritising effective thinking. Without the awareness of how you think, you limit your ability to challenge any self-limiting beliefs and replace them with self-empowering ones.

By addressing an ineffective mindset, you set into motion the process for personal growth, enhanced well-being, improved problem-solving, and greater success in both your personal and professional life.

> Q: What ineffective thinking or behaviour gets in the way of you reaching your professional or personal goals or being effective?
>
> -> Self-doubt?
>
> -> Catastrophising?
>
> -> All-or-nothing thinking?
>
> -> Overgeneralisation?
>
> -> Self-criticism?
>
> -> Mind reading?
>
> -> Personalisation?
>
> -> Should statements?
>
> -> Filtering?
>
> -> Discounting the positive (Imposter syndrome)?
>
> -> Other?

#2: The STOP Method

Now that you have identified your ineffective thinking, the next step is to STOP it. Unless, of course, you want to continue with self-doubt, catastrophising, self-criticism, or discounting the positive, which I doubt.

Stopping your ineffective thought processing involves mindfulness. You need to be sufficiently aware of what's going on inside your mind before you can do something about it. You need to shine the light of attention into the darkened corners of your mind and illuminate your mental space so you can see what's going on.

You can't do this with a cluttered mind. You need to do some spring cleaning and clear out the mental nooks and crannies that you have been neglecting and putting aside.

So, yes, you need to practice mindfulness, which is:

> *A mental state characterised by present-moment awareness and non-judgemental observation, often cultivated through practices like meditation.*

Mindfulness involves deliberately paying attention to your thoughts, feelings, bodily sensations, and the surrounding environment without trying to change or judge them.

But why bother? Well, mindfulness is widely recognised for its positive effects on mental and emotional well-being. There's ample research to show that mindfulness can help reduce stress and anxiety, improve emotional well-being, and enhance overall mental clarity and resilience.

It also encourages a non-reactive and accepting approach to the thoughts and experiences that arise, allowing for a deeper understanding of yourself and the world around you. Including your ineffective thinking.

So how does mindfulness work?

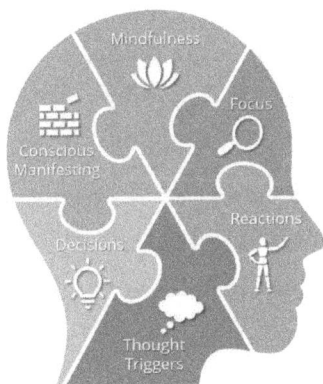

FIGURE 11: The Process of Mindfulness

The above figure is a visual representation of the life-changing process of mindfulness and how it works:

-> Mindfulness gives laser-sharp focus on the here and now, limiting worries of the future and minimising regrets and judgements of the past.

-> This sharpened focus leads to greater awareness of how you are reacting and behaving, which increases your insight into your thought triggers of your emotions.

-> This insight clears your mind of the emotional clutter that hampers good decision-making, and once you make better decisions and choices you are then able to consciously manifest the results you desire.

This is *life-changing*, as bestselling authors like Jack Canfield, Jim Rohn, Zig Ziglar, and Earl Nightingale tell us, because your thoughts are creating your reality.

> *When you change your thinking, you literally change the way you experience the world.*

So, to get the maximum practical benefits of mindfulness, I advise you to create the habit of every 90-minutes to STOP!

-> **S**: Stop what you're doing.

-> **T**: Take a breath.

-> **O**: Observe your body.

-> **P**: Proceed.

This is 'The STOP Method', and it is perhaps the easiest mindfulness technique you can do. You can literally STOP anytime and anywhere.

At the traffic lights. Washing the dishes. Waiting for the kettle to boil. Typing an email. Sitting on the bus... or on the toilet.

There are no excuses. This method doesn't ask you to spend thirty minutes a day meditating. It doesn't ask you to sit in uncomfortable positions. It doesn't ask you to isolate yourself from everyone else in a dark room. None of that.

All it asks is that whenever you remember, take 15 seconds to stop what you're doing, take a breath, observe your body, and then proceed with what you were doing.

Mindfulness doesn't get any easier than that.

Q: So when and where are you going to STOP?

#3: Effective Self-Talk

You've now taken the first two steps to prioritise effective thinking. You have identified your ineffective thinking, and you have learned how to put a STOP to it. The next step is to neutralise your ineffective thinking by reframing your negative thoughts with a positive thought.

This is where the strategy of 'Inserting the But' comes in. You will remember how we used this strategy to break through procrastination in *Chapter 8* by nullifying the unhelpful conclusions that arise from excuse-making and 'Inserting the But' to develop more helpful conclusions.

When used to neutralise the negative self-talk that arises from ineffective thinking, the principle is the same.

For instance, the ineffective mindset of 'self-doubt' can be paralysing, preventing you from taking action and pursuing your goals. Here you need to challenge your self-doubt through self-confidence by 'Inserting the But' so that you can get unstuck and start moving forward toward your goals.

Another ineffective mindset, that of 'personalisation', involves unfairly assuming blame for external events and outcomes, which can lead to unnecessary guilt and stress. Here you need to reframe this thought pattern through self-compassion by also 'Inserting the But' so that you begin accepting that you're not at fault for every external occurrence and that you can only control your own actions and reactions.

Let's now discuss some examples of how 'Inserting the But' can help you neutralise ineffective thinking and negative self-talk.

-> Self-Doubt:

Negative self-talk: "I'll never be able to succeed in this new job. I don't have the skills or experience."

Positive self-talk: "BUT... I can always ask for more training and supervision while I work so I can build my skills and experience."

-> Catastrophising:

Negative self-talk: "If I don't ace this presentation, my entire career will be ruined."

Positive self-talk: "BUT... even if I don't do so well, there will always be another opportunity to put myself forward and advance my career."

-> All-or-Nothing:

Negative self-talk: "If I can't commit to working out for an hour every day, there's no point in even trying to get in shape."

Positive self-talk: "BUT... fitness and health is a marathon, not a sprint, and each step no matter how small is a step in the right direction."

-> Overgeneralisation:

Negative self-talk: "I messed up that report, so I'm terrible at my job and always will be."

Positive self-talk: "BUT... I am learning to be more accepting of my mistakes and learning to use them as stepping-stones to my success."

-> Self-Criticism:

Negative self-talk: "I'm such a failure. I can't do anything right, and I'll never be successful."

Positive self-talk: "BUT... I choose to focus on 'The Strength in Me' and not my weaknesses, as that is the path to success."

-> Mind Reading:

Negative self-talk: "I just know my coworkers are talking behind my back and criticising my work."

Positive self-talk: "BUT... I don't have ESP, so there's no point in second-guessing myself. What's more, what other people think of me is none of my business."

-> Personalisation:

Negative self-talk: "It's my fault that the project failed. I should have done more to prevent it."

Positive self-talk: "BUT... I'm not responsible for the entire world, only for myself. I accept responsibility for my actions or inaction, but not for others.'"

-> Should Statements:

Negative self-talk: "I should be working late every night to prove my dedication to the company."

Positive self-talk: "BUT... I choose to prioritise my own mental, emotional, and physical health, otherwise I could suffer burnout."

-> Filtering:

Negative self-talk: "Despite all the praise I received for my presentation, I can't stop thinking about the one person who didn't seem impressed."

Positive self-talk: "BUT... although I'd like everyone to praise and like me, that's not realistic. I choose to focus on those who value and support me, not those who don't see my value."

-> Discounting the Positive:

Negative self-talk: "Sure, I got a promotion, but it was probably just luck. I'm not really that capable."

Positive self-talk: "BUT... I will not listen to the imposter in my mind, I will strengthen the voice of positivity by listening to it instead."

Q: Describe how you can neutralise negative self-talk in the following scenarios:

-> Self-doubt?

-> Catastrophising?

-> All-or-nothing thinking?

-> Overgeneralisation?

-> Self-criticism?

-> Mind reading?

-> Personalisation?

-> Should statements?

-> Filtering?

-> Discounting the positive (Imposter syndrome)?

#4: Effective Value

Once you've identified your ineffective thinking, put a STOP to it, and then neutralised your ineffective thinking with effective self-talk, focusing on your Effective Value (EV) is the final step to prioritising effective thinking.

If you're wondering what Effective Value is, here's the key:

> *You can't think effectively if you only think about yourself.*

People who are self-centred and self-focused are not effective. If you only think about what you want, what you are feeling, what you do, what you need, then you limit your effectiveness to only one person, you. Your Effective Value is minimal when you only consider yourself.

But when you include others in your thinking, when you include others in your quest for success and happiness, then your Effective Value rises. In other words,

> *The value of your effectiveness—your EV—is directly proportional to your desire to help other people.*

Motivational speaker and international bestselling author, Zig Ziglar, believed that helping others is the key to success and happiness. He believed that you could get anything you want in life as long as you helped enough people get what they want.

In his book, *Happiness to Live By: 100 Inspiring Stories to Smile About*,[20] he said this about the power of helping others:

> *The only way to reach the mountain peaks of life is to forget about self and help other people reach greater heights.*

Helping others achieve their goals is therefore the essence of Effective Value, the definition of which is this:

> *Effective Value is the level to which you consciously serve the continuous advancement and development of all humankind.*

Let's now dissect this definition of Effective Value into its components so we can appreciate its importance.

Effective Value is to be Value-Able

To have Effective Value is to be a person of mutual value to others and to one's self, and for that value to be a consciously effective force aiding the progress and continual advancement of all, for the benefit of all, at the expense of no-one.

A diamond undiscovered beneath the ground has potential value, but it does not as yet have Effective Value because nobody knows it exists.

Only when that diamond is discovered, cut, polished, and offered to others for their benefit does it shift its value from

---

[20] Zig Ziglar, *Happiness to Live By: 100 Inspiring Stories to Smile About*, Thomas Nelson, 2023

a gem with hidden potential to that which is effective and value-*able*.

> Tip: That hidden gem within you is your love for humanity—your desire for others to have that which you want for yourself, life in abundance.

It is incumbent on you to discover that gem and bring it to the surface of your consciousness. Then, when you polish that gem and offer it to others for their benefit, you enable your value by transforming it from that which was hidden to that which is now effective and value-able.

You will rise to become a person of Effective Value and your life will reap the rewards of being value-able.

Effective Value is a Level of Conscious Service

The degree to which you intentionally and willingly serve others for mutual benefit is a direct measure of your value to the world. That is, your level of Effective Value.

Those who are self-serving and treat everyone as a resource for their own benefit have little or no Effective Value. They are the takers of the world with no thought for others apart from what they can get for themselves.

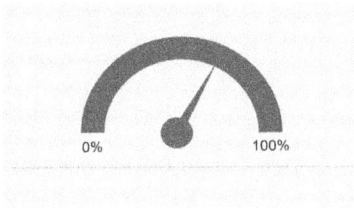

FIGURE 12:   Effective Value Gauge

Those who serve others but are self-sacrificing to their own detriment do have Effective Value, but because they ignore their own needs and well-being, they only attain a modicum of Effective Value. Although they are the givers of the world, it comes at great personal cost.

Effective Value requires balance. You are here to enjoy your life and your time here on this planet, not suffer it. So those with high Effective Value are those who look after others and themselves with equal measure.

> Tip: A useful way to move the pointer higher on the Effective Value Gauge is to view every moment as an opportunity to serve others for each others' mutual benefit.

Know, then, the importance of following the Golden Rule in everything you do and it will keep you in good stead to increase your level of Effective Value:

> *Do unto others that which you would have them do unto you.*

Effective Value Advances and Develops All Humankind

When the use of your talents and gifts is limited only for your own benefit and success, then whatever success you achieve will represent the limit of your potential and capability.

Your Effective Value is therefore minimised and limited when all you do is focus on what you can get for yourself—to focus solely on you and what you can gain from others is to put limits on yourself. So why do it?

But when you use your talents and gifts for the benefit and success for all humankind, whatever success you achieve will no longer represent the limits of your potential and capability, rather it will be the launchpad for even greater success and achievement.

This is because your Effective Value is actually limitless. So when everything you think, say, and do is dedicated to the advancement and development of each and everyone (which includes yourself as part of the greater whole, just not limited to you and only you), you cannot fail to tap into your limitless Effective Value and become a person of unlimited success.

> Tip: 'Advancement and development' is akin to mental, physical, emotional, material, and spiritual progress and evolution, so that all may experience the fullness of life.

In their heart of hearts, those with the highest levels of Effective Value are those who desire for others everything that they desire for themselves—health, wealth, well-being, happiness, self-determination, love—and for everyone to have all this in abundance at the expense of no-one.

It is to have a win-win, non-competitive mindset, to crave success for all without disadvantaging anyone else. To know and believe deeply that:

> *Success isn't reliant upon taking from another; rather, success is the attainment of the fullness of life for all.*

That fullness isn't the collation and attainment of material riches; money, power, posessions, which many seek and compete for, but few obtain. These are but transient and temporary.

Rather, it is something more permanent and enriching—the abundant wealth of joy, peace, freedom, love, health, well-being, wisdom, and belonging that you experience when you immerse yourself in the Flow of Life.

This is the priceless value of effective thinking.

> Q: What can you do now to focus on your Effective Value and prioritise effective thinking in each of your 7 Life Segments?
>
> -> Family & Relationships?
>
> -> Career & Work?
>
> -> Money & Finances?
>
> -> Health & Wellbeing?
>
> -> Learning & Education?
>
> -> Fun & Adventure?
>
> -> Spirituality & Ethics?

Main Points:

1. What you give your attention to becomes your conscious reality.
2. The average person has 3-17 million negative thoughts per year, and 1.36 billion in a lifetime.
3. Imagine the person who has 1.36 billion *positive* thoughts in their lifetime.
4. Mindfulness is a mental state characterised by present-moment awareness and non-judgemental observation, often cultivated through practices like meditation.
5. When you change your thinking, you literally change the way you experience the world.
6. Effective Value (EV) is the level to which you consciously serve the continuous advancement and development of all humankind.
7. The Golden Rule: Do unto others that which you would have them do unto you.
8. Success isn't reliant upon taking from another; rather, success is the attainment of the fullness of life for all.

PART 3

STRATEGIES

TO IMPROVE

CAPABILITY

& CAPACITY

12 EFFECTIVE ENERGY-MANAGEMENT

'Energy and persistence conquer all things.'
Benjamin Franklin

THE EFFECTIVENESS EQUATION—$E = MC^2$—stresses the importance of mindset, capability, and capacity in maintaining and sustaining your personal and professional effectiveness.

This is because it isn't circumstances or your environment that determines whether you are effective or ineffective—it's *how you think* and what you focus on.

> *Circumstances do not make or break who you are*
> *—they reveal who you are.*

What's inside you will come out when you're put to the test. The real you will be expressed in moments of high pressure. As we've said before, when you squeeze an orange, you get orange juice. When you squeeze a lemon, you get lemon juice.

What you express when you are squeezed is a product of what you are focusing on in that moment. Your words, emotions, and behaviours—your 'juice'—flow from your consciousness, what you are putting your attention on.

Do you focus on the glass half-full or half-empty? Do you worry about problems you can't control or focus on the things you can control? Do you blame others or events for where you are now, or do you take responsibility for where you are and where you want to be?

Effective people aren't people without problems: they are people who have learned to effectively solve their problems. They are solution-focused, not problem-focused.

They have learned to focus on strategies to improve their self-management because these strategies are the processes by which they improve their personal and professional effectiveness.

Capability & Capacity

As we have discussed in great length the critical role that your mindset plays in your effectiveness, the following chapters will now discuss the importance of capability and capacity.

Whatever limits your capability or capacity limits your effectiveness. Whatever expands your capability or capacity expands your effectiveness.

We will therefore focus on identifying what decreases your capability or capacity and what you can do about it, as well as discussing strategies you can use to increase your capability and capacity. Which, again, comes down to good self-management.

As such, there are three important areas of self-management that you can address to increase your capability and capacity:

1. Effective Energy-Management.

2. Effective Time-Management.

3. Effective Goal-Setting.

ENERGY-MANAGEMENT

Your mental, emotional, and physical energy levels play a big role in maintaining and sustaining your overall effectiveness.

If you are mentally, emotionally, and physically exhausted, your capability and capacity is severely affected. Anything that drains your energy and leaves you feeling flat and depleted will have knock-on effects on your personal and professional effectiveness.

If you simply don't have the mental, emotional, or physical capacity to do anything, you won't do it. Or, if you do try to do it, you will only do it half-heartedly and give up at the slightest difficulty.

On the flipside, anything that boosts your mental, emotional, and physical energy levels boosts your capability and capacity and thus your overall effectiveness.

You will be filled with conviction and self-belief (mental energy), you will be filled with enthusiasm and excitement (emotional energy), and you will be filled with vitality and zest (physical energy).

Who can stop you when you feel like this?

Personal Energy-Management

As we have learned, the focus of your attention determines your effectiveness. Your thoughts are powerful because with them you create your world.

Your thoughts are the only thing over which you have 100% control. How you think, what you believe, how you reason, are all subject to your control. You are the master of your mind.

You are therefore the master of your experience. What happens to you is not nearly as important as to what happens inside your mind.

What you focus on, you internalise and observe. What you choose to focus on therefore determines your experience. This also includes your emotions and your personal energy levels. The choice is yours.

Personal energy-management is such a choice. Of course, you need to make good choices for healthy eating, exercise, and sleep. But this discussion is not about eating the right foods, making sure you do your 10,000 steps a day, or getting a good night's rest. The assumption is that you already know this.

Rather, our discussion on personal energy-management will focus on the choices you make that support and sustain your energy, vitality, productivity, and peace.

The choices you make to feel more lively and active depend on what you focus on. For instance, if you focus on negativity and what you can't and won't do, then diminishing energy levels and decreased effectiveness will be your experience.

If you focus on positivity and what you can and will do, then renewed energy and increased effectiveness will be your experience.

So let's discuss how you can renew your energy through focus.

The Energy-Management Matrix

This graph is a visual demonstration of how people with good self-management identify areas in which they can improve their mental, emotional, and physical energy levels.

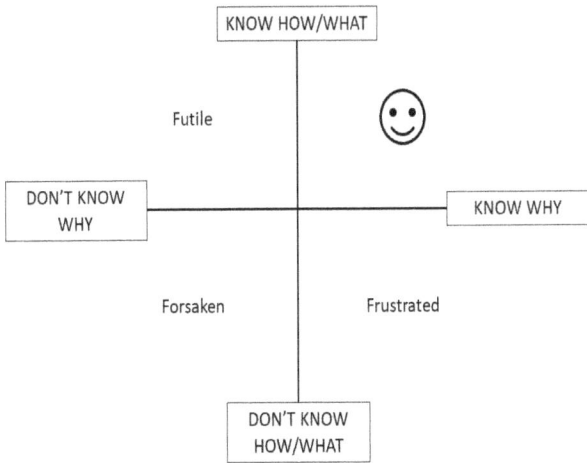

FIGURE 13:   Energy-Management Matrix

The Energy-Management Matrix is divided into four quadrants based on knowledge and purpose. On the vertical axis, you either have the knowledge of how or what you want to achieve or become, or you don't have that knowledge.

On the horizontal axis, you either have the clarity or the understanding of your purpose, the reason 'why' you do what you do or what you want to become, or you don't have that clarity of purpose.

Let's discuss these four quadrants and how they affect your personal energy-management.

Quadrant #1

The top right quadrant is the 'happy place' where you are full of self-belief, enthusiasm, and vitality.

Here you know how or what you want to do and you have clarity of the purpose for doing it. You feel you have the capability and the capacity to do anything you set your mind to. You feel fantastic.

This is the place where we all want to be, the quadrant of good energy-management.

Quadrant #2

The top left quadrant is a quadrant of low mental energy, where you know how or what you need to do but you don't know why. In this quadrant you lack *purpose*.

When you lack purpose and you are just going through the motions, what you do seems futile. It doesn't matter what you do, even if you do it well, there's no point. It doesn't matter. It isn't important.

The sense of futility is mentally draining, so what you need to do if you find yourself in this quadrant is to focus on finding your sense of purpose.

Finding your reason 'why' will increase your mental capacity because it will revitalise your mindset and reinvigorate your self-belief.

Purpose is your focus in this quadrant.

Quadrant #3

The bottom right quadrant is a quadrant of low emotional energy, where you actually do have clarity of your purpose, why you are doing what you are doing, but you don't have the knowledge or skills to complete it. In this quadrant you lack the *know-how* to do it.

When you believe in the purpose of what you're doing but lack the resources to see it into fruition, what you are doing feels incredibly frustrating. You can see the port you wish to sail to but you don't know how to get there. You feel like a ship becalmed at sea. You pull your hair out. You get angry. You throw your hands in the air in exasperation.

This sense of frustration is emotionally draining, so what you need to do if you find yourself in this quadrant is to focus on the resources you need to get the job done. This includes upskilling, training, re-educating, learning, and seeking help.

When you have the know-how to do what you want to do and become what you want to be, you will feel more capable of achieving your goals. Your frustration will then make way for greater confidence and enthusiasm.

You will start to feel that excitement for life once again.

Quadrant #4

The bottom left quadrant is a quadrant of low mental energy and low emotional energy, where you don't know how or what you need to do and you don't know why you need to do anything either.

In this quadrant you lack know-how *and* purpose.

When you lack know-how and purpose at the same time, you feel not only are you just going through the motions but that there is no escape from it either. This is as good as it gets. This is your lot in life, and there's not much you can do about it. You can feel completely forsaken.

The sense of forsakenness is mentally, emotionally, and even physically draining. It's actually very debilitating. So what you need to do if you find yourself in this quadrant is to focus on finding your *sense of self.*

You have to 'find yourself' again, the real you, the you that you've forgotten. The you that's gotten lost in the mayhem and craziness of everyday life. The you that once had great enthusiasm, excitement, and vitality for life.

You have to get back to basics. You have to work out what you really want out of life—your goals, ambitions, passions, desires—because only then, only once you know what you want and what you want to become, can you work out how to achieve it and understand the purpose behind it.

Only then will you have the energy to push forward and progress toward the happy quadrant.

> Q: What quadrant in the Energy-Management Matrix do you identify with at the moment? What do you need to do to get to Quadrant #1, the 'happy quadrant'?

REBOOT #1: ENERGY DRAINS

In life, there are certain things that drain our energy and leave us feeling depleted and exhausted, thus making us less effective.

Your energy can leak, weakening your capability and capacity, so it's important to identify where those energy leaks occur and prevent them from recurring.

Such things can be people, situations, work, places, events, certain times of the year, even your own thoughts.

With this in mind, we will now discuss the personal energy-management strategy that I call 'Reboot', which will focus on minimising your energy drains and boosting your energy fuels in each of your 7 Life Segments.

> Q: Rate your energy-management in each of your 7 Life Segments on a scale of 0-10 (where 0 is lowest and 10 is highest).

> Q: Rank each of your 7 Life Segments in order of *highest energy levels* (1-7) and give your reasons for each ranking.

Reducing Your Energy Drains

We will now consider each of your 7 Life Segments and identify any energy drains that may be present. Once you have identified these energy drains, the next step is to work out which Energy-Management Matrix quadrant your energy drains fit into.

Once you know what quadrant you are dealing with, you can then establish a plan or 'workaround' to reduce your energy drains.

This is how to get yourself out of that quadrant and into the 'happy quadrant', and here's an example of how this strategy works:

> -> Life Segment: Family & Relationships
>
> -> Energy Drain: There is someone I need to forgive.
>
> -> Quadrant #3: I know I need to forgive them but I don't see why I should be the one to give in to them after what they did to me.
>
> -> Resolution: 'Finding My Why'. Forgiveness will help me to let go of my anger and humiliation, emotions that are draining my energy and holding me back from moving forward. I will forgive them for my benefit, not necessarily for their benefit.

As you can see, the Energy-Management Matrix is a powerful tool to help you stop the energy bleed and begin the process to recover and re-energise. Here's another example of how it works:

> -> Life Segment: Money & Finances
>
> -> Energy Drain: I have debt that needs to be paid off.
>
> -> Quadrant #2: I just don't know how I'm going to pay my debts.

-> Resolution: 'Get Some Help'. There are plenty of financial advisors and debt-management companies I can ask for help. They can teach me how to set up a plan for debt repayment over the next 6 to 12 months and help clear my debts.

Finally, one more example of how this energy-management strategy works before you give it a go:

-> Life Segment: Spirituality & Ethics

-> Energy Drain: I have let slip a spiritual or religious practice that used to give me a sense of purpose in my life.

-> Quadrant #4: I'm so time-poor that I wouldn't know where to begin, nor am I convinced it would do any good.

-> Resolution: 'Reconnecting My Power'. I do remember that having a sense of higher purpose used to fill me with energy and passion. I need to reconnect with that higher power because without this connection I am like a lightbulb disconnected from electricity—I cannot shine without connecting to my power source.

You will have many energy drains in each of your 7 Life Segments, from relationship squabbles to financial concerns, to health issues, to needing a holiday. My advice is for you to identify as many energy drains as you can and devise a plan or 'workaround' to reduce these energy drains using the Energy-Management Matrix.

You are invited to download a free PDF checklist of 'energy drains' from my website to help you identify and reduce your energy drains.[21]

Go through each of the 7 Life Segments in this checklist and tick each statement that is relevant to you. This checklist will help you identify your main energy drains.

> Q: Identify your 'energy drains' for each of your 7 Life Segments. Choose your top priority item in each Life Segment that you would most like to handle now:
>
> 1.   5.
> 2.   6.
> 3.   7.
> 4.

> Q: Using the Energy-Management Matrix, write down how you plan to *reduce* your energy drains for each of your 7 Life Segments over the next 21 days:
>
> 1.   5.
> 2.   6.
> 3.   7.
> 4.

---

[21] Readers can download a free Energy-Drain PDF checklist by visiting my website at www.scottzarcinas.com/energy-drains

REBOOT #2: ENERGY FUELS

Just as there are certain things in life that seem to drain our energy and leave us feeling depleted and exhausted, there are things that also boost our energy supplies and add to our fuel, leaving us feeling invigorated and alive.

Like energy drains, energy fuels can be people, situations, work, places, events, certain times of the year, even your own thoughts.

Boosting Your Energy Fuels

We will now consider each of your 7 Life Segments and identify any energy boosts that you can use. All energy boosts are aligned with Quadrant #1 in the Energy-Management Matrix.

All that's required is for you to identify the know-how and the purpose of each energy boost, and implement a plan to regularly boost your energy.

This is how to keep re-energised in the 'happy quadrant' and maintain good energy-management, and here's an example of how this strategy works:

-> Life Segment: Family & Relationships

-> Energy Fuel: I enjoy and value the company of special friends.

-> Quadrant #1: Identify which friends energise me and their value to me.

-> Resolution: 'Maintaining Positive Friendships'. My friends support me and make me laugh but sometimes weeks and months go by without seeing them. I resolve to meeting up with my special friends at least once a month and will make this a priority.

As you can see, the Energy-Management Matrix is not just a powerful tool to help you stop your energy drains, but also a great tool to boost your energy fuels and re-energise. Here's another example of how it works:

-> Life Segment: Learning & Education

-> Energy Fuel: I love reading books.

-> Quadrant #1: Identify which books I like to read and which ones I most enjoy.

-> Resolution: 'My Bucket List Books'. Sometimes life gets in the way and I don't have the time or mental bandwidth to pick up a book and read. In fact, the last time I read was on holiday. But I love a good book and enjoy immersing myself in the story, so I will create a bucket list of 'must read' books I have always wanted to read and set a goal of reading three books per year.

Finally, one more example of how this energy-management strategy works before you give it a go:

-> Life Segment: Fun & Adventure

-> Energy Fuel: I love to travel and go on holidays.

-> Quadrant #1: Identify which destinations I like to go and which ones I feel most relaxed.

-> Resolution: 'My Weekend Getaways'. The cost of living has meant that I don't have as much savings for holidays as I'd like. But I still feel refreshed and energised going away even if it's just for the weekend, so I will make a list of 'weekend getaways' that are in my budget and book a place to stay eight times a year.

Just as you have many energy drains in each of your 7 Life Segments, you will also have many energy fuels, from meaningful friendships to financial goals to hobbies to watching movies.

My advice is for you to identify as many energy fuels as you can and devise a plan to boost these energy fuels using the Energy-Management Matrix.

You are invited to download a free PDF checklist of 'energy fuels' from my website to help you identify and boost your energy fuels.[22]

Go through each of the 7 Life Segments in this checklist and tick each statement that is relevant to you. This checklist will help you identify your main energy fuels.

---

[22] Readers can download a free Energy-Fuels PDF checklist by visiting my website at www.scottzarcinas.com/energy-fuels

Q: Identify your 'energy fuels' for each of your 7 Life Segments. Choose your top priority item in each Life Segment that you would most like to handle now:

1.   5.

2.   6.

3.   7.

4.

Q: Write down how you plan to *boost* your energy fuels for each of your 7 Life Segments over the next 21 days:

1.   5.

2.   6.

3.   7.

4.

Main Points:

1. Circumstances do not make or break who you are —they reveal who you are.

2. What you choose to focus on will determine your effectiveness and your experience. The choice is yours.

3. Anything that boosts your mental, emotional, and physical energy levels boosts your capability and capacity and thus your overall effectiveness.

4. What drains your energy limits your effectiveness.

5. What fuels your energy boosts your effectiveness.

6. The Energy-Management Matrix is a visual demonstration of how people with good self-management identify areas in which they can improve their mental, emotional, and physical energy levels.

7. The Energy-Management Matrix is divided into four quadrants based on knowledge and purpose.

8. The personal energy-management strategy of 'Reboot' involves identifying your energy drains and energy fuels in your 7 Life Segments.

13 EFFECTIVE TIME-MANAGEMENT

'The key is in not spending time, but in investing it.'

Stephen R. Covey

JUST AS YOUR personal energy-management plays a big role in maintaining and sustaining your overall effectiveness, so too does your personal time-management.

As we have discussed, anything that drains your energy and leaves you feeling flat and depleted will have knock-on effects because it limits your capability and capacity to function well.

On the flipside, anything that boosts your energy levels also boosts your capability and capacity to function well, and thus boosts your overall effectiveness.

Likewise, good time-management increases your capability and capacity to function well, whereas poor time-management decreases your capability and capacity to function well.

For instance, if you are a poor time-manager you will ignore or miss the chance to invest the time to learn new skills (capability) or to improve your productivity (capacity). In the work environment, failure to increase your capability and capacity may result in opportunities for career advancement passing you by.

Furthermore, in the relentless pursuit of success, it's easy to overlook the toll that poor time management can take on your well-being. Chronic stress, caused by the never-ending pressure to meet deadlines and juggle multiple responsibilities, can erode your physical and mental health.

> *Time-management isn't just about clock-watching or creating endless to-do lists; it's a fundamental skill that enables you to maximise your productivity, reduce stress, tackle unforeseen challenges, seize opportunities, and achieve your goals with greater efficiency.*

Good time-management is therefore a good way to improve your overall effectiveness and thereby escape the flea circus.

The Currency of Success

Time is an invaluable and finite resource that we all share, regardless of our backgrounds, professions, or age. How you manage this resource can significantly impact every area of your life.

We are inundated with demands and distractions almost every minute of the day, so the ability to master time-management is a defining factor that sets high-achievers apart from the rest.

We all have the same 24 hours in a day, but successful people manage their time more effectively than those who are less successful.

In our professional lives, for instance, time-management is the cornerstone of productivity. It's the mechanism with which you allocate your time with good care, ensuring that the most critical tasks and objectives are given the attention they deserve.

Whether you're a top executive, an entrepreneur, a freelancer, or a student, your effectiveness hinges on how well you can make the most of your hours and minutes.

Time is often referred to as the 'currency of success.' This is because time is a finite and diminishing asset, which makes it extraordinarily valuable. Like any currency, what you invest your time in grows and appreciates. Which is why time is best appreciated as an investment and not an expenditure.

It is also why you shouldn't spend time to save money; you should rather spend money to save time. Then use that time you have 'saved' to invest in the things that make your life more fulfilling and meaningful.

As Thomas Edison, inventor and founder of General Electric, is often quoted as saying,

> *Time is really the only capital that any human being has, and the only thing he can't afford to lose.*

Yet the flow of time is beyond anyone's control; irrespective of anything you do, time keeps ticking. What you can control, however, is how you manage yourself in the time that you have.

So the best time-managers are the best self-managers. But time-management is not limited to boardroom meetings and project deadlines; it extends to your personal life as well.

Effective time-management directly impacts the quality of your personal relationships, your physical and mental well-being, and the pursuit of your passions and interests.

The balance between personal and professional life is a constant challenge, and successful individuals recognise that optimising their time enables them to excel in both worlds.

That's the true currency of success.

> Q: How do you currently manage your time? What are some time-management tips or strategies that work for you now?

Time-Management Strategies

Although there are many time-management strategies (and hence, self-management strategies), we will discuss the top four strategies that I believe have the most impact on how you can best manage your time.

These four strategies are best remembered as **TIME**:

Time Audit

Itemise the Day

Most Important Tasks

Exclude Non-Essentials

We will discuss these time-management strategies first and then briefly list some time-management tools that will help you to implement these strategies.

T: TIME-AUDIT

As Thomas Edison said, time is the only thing we can't afford to lose. Which is why we need to be mindful of our time-stealers and time-wasters and minimise any loss of time.

> *Effective time-managers know where their time goes. They don't have a vague idea. They know exactly, and they actively work on eliminating their time-stealers and time-wasters.*

To find out where you are spending your time, a good idea is to keep a time log for 2-4 days, including at least one weekend day and one week day. The results will surprise you.

So let's not waste time. Begin your time audit now with what you have been doing up until this moment, and then continue the audit tonight and tomorrow.

You are invited to download a free 24-hour Time Audit PDF from my website to help you identify time-stealers and time-wasters and better manage your time.[23]

---

[23] Readers can download a 24-hour Time Audit PDF by visiting my website at www.scottzarcinas.com/time-audit

TIME	ACTIVITY
6.00-7.00am	
7.00-8.00am	
8.00-8.30am	
8.30-9.00am	
9.00-9.15am	
9.15-9.30am	
9.30-9.45am	
9.45-10.00am	
10.00-10.15am	
10.15-10.30am	
10.30-10.45am	
10.45-11.00am	
11.00-11.15am	
11.30-11.45am	
12.00-12.15am	
12.15-12.30pm	
12.30-12.45pm	
1.00-1.15pm	
1.15-1.30pm	
1.30-1.45pm	
1.45-2.00pm	
2.00-2.15pm	
2.15-2.30pm	
2.30-2.45pm	
2.45-3.00pm	
3.00-3.15pm	
3.15-3.30pm	

TIME	ACTIVITY
3.30.3.45pm	
3.45.4.00pm	
4.00-4.15pm	
4.15-4.30pm	
4.30-4.45pm	
4.45-5.00pm	
5.00-5.15pm	
5.15-5.30pm	
5.30-5.45pm	
5.45-6.00pm	
6.00-6.15pm	
6.15-6.30pm	
6.30-6.45pm	
6.45-7.00pm	
7.00-7.15pm	
7.30-7.45pm	
7.45-8.00pm	
8.00-8.15pm	
8.15-8.30pm	
8.30-8.45pm	
8.45-9.00pm	
9.00-9.15pm	
9.15-9.30pm	
9.30-9.45pm	
9.45-10.00pm	
10.00-10.45pm	
11.00-12.00pm	

Keeping track of your time with a time log is an important first step in identifying where you might be losing time.

> Q: Consider your 7 Life Segments and rate your time-management in each of them on a scale of 0-10 (where 0 is lowest and 10 is highest).

> Q: Rank your 7 Life Segments in order of biggest *time wastage*. Give your reason for each ranking.

The second step is to eliminate any time-stealers and time-wasters that have been flagged in your time log.

The best way to do this is to make a list of your personal and professional time-stealers and time-wasters:

> Q: What are your top time-stealers and time-wasters in each of your 7 Life Segments?

Now identify one time-stealer or time-waster in each Life Segment that you are committed to eliminate.

> Q: How will you eliminate this time-stealer or time-waster? State your action plan over the next week for each of your 7 Life Segments.
>
> -> Family & Relationships?
>
> -> Career & Work?
>
> -> Money & Finances?
>
> -> Health & Wellbeing?
>
> -> Learning & Education?
>
> -> Fun & Adventure?
>
> -> Spirituality & Ethics?

I: ITEMISE THE DAY

The second time-management strategy, *Itemise the Day*, involves these steps:

1. Write down everything you need to do.
2. Plan ahead (last thing/first thing).
3. Number the items in order of what needs doing (first to last).
4. Proceed with the first item until it's completed.

> Tip: Don't over-plan the day. For instance, include in your plan some buffer time either side of your tasks so that it won't cause undue stress if you go over time with some tasks.

Earl Nightingale, motivational speaker and author of the bestselling book and audiobook, *The Strangest Secret*,[24] often made mention of what he called, 'The $25,000 Idea'.

The story is about how a man was paid $25,000 for one single idea. Not bad for 30 minutes' work. Here is an adapted version of Nightingale's story from the transcript of his audio presentation.

The $25,000 Idea

Ivy Lee was an efficiency expert in the post-World War 2 era who offered valuable advice to the president of a small American steel company seeking improved management.

---

[24] Earl Nightingale, *The Strangest Secret: How to live the life you desire*, Nightingale Conant, 1957 (audio)

The president acknowledged gaps in his management of the company, but what he wanted from Lee wasn't more knowledge, rather "a lot more doing" and "a better way of getting things done".

He then added that he'd pay Lee anything he asked, within reason. So Lee promised to boost the company's efficiency by 50% in just twenty minutes.

Lee then instructed the president to jot down the six most critical tasks for the next day and rank them by importance to him or the company.

The president was to begin with the top item, focusing solely on it until completion, and then proceed to the next. But only when the first item was completed, not before. He was to follow this method for all six items on the list.

Lee stressed that if this method didn't complete all tasks, no other approach would, but it would save considerable time and prioritise tasks in order of importance.

He then left, telling the president to have his people try this system for as long as he liked. Then, when the president was convinced of the value of this idea, he was to send him a cheque for whatever he thought it was worth to the company.

The interview lasted no more than 30 minutes. In a few weeks, the company's president sent Lee a cheque for $25,000, deeming it the most profitable lesson he had ever learned.

Within five years, the company's transformation into one of the world's major independent steel producers was largely attributed to this simple, yet highly effective, time-management technique.

> *The $25,00 Idea:*
> *Taking things one at a time in their proper order and staying with one task until its successful completion before going on to the next.*

So let's try the $25,000 idea for yourself over the next 7 days and see how effective it can be in your personal and professional life.

Q: Tonight, write down the six most important things you have to do. Then number them in the order of their importance. Tomorrow, go to work on number 1. Continue with it untill it's successfully completed, then move on to number 2, and so on. When you've finished with all six, get another piece of paper and repeat the process.

Successfully handling each task to the degree of the importance of the tasks is the key, which we will elaborate on in the next time-management strategy, *Most Important Tasks*.

Successfully doing a lot of unnecessary things actually falls into your time-waster category.

So it's important that the tasks you do efficiently are actually important tasks, tasks that propel you steadily toward your goal.

Tip: Remember that you do not need to worry about tomorrow or the next day, or what's going to happen at the end of the month. You only need to focus on what you are doing now, today, in this moment.

Effectiveness is built one day at a time. Each task handled successfully will help you circumnavigate every obstacle and solve every problem.

> *Successful tasks make successful days.*
> *Successful days build a successful life.*

'Itemising the Day' is a simple but tremendously powerful idea that has the potential to remove much of the confusion in your life and bring order and effectiveness into it.

You'll stop running around in circles wondering what to do next. And you'll be surprised at the speed with which you will accomplish the things that need doing, and in the order of their importance.

M: MOST IMPORTANT TASKS

The third time-management strategy, *Most Important Tasks*, involves two main steps:

1. Prioritasking—do important things first.

2. Batching—do similar tasks together.

Prioritasking

Motivational speaker and bestselling author of *Eat that Frog!*,[25] Brian Tracy, talks of a procrastination-busting strategy whereby you do the most unpleasant thing you need to do first thing in the morning so that it's done and you do not procrastinate throughout the day.

The strategy of 'prioritasking' is a similar time-management strategy whereby:

> *You do the most important tasks first.*

Your most important task might also be your most unpleasant thing you need to do, which is the 'horrible frog' that Tracy says you must 'eat first' and get it over and done with.

But even if it isn't, get it done as soon as you possibly can and you will be rest assured throughout the day that you have already done not only the most unpleasant task, but also the most important task. You then have the rest of the day knowing the worst is over!

The 4 D's 'prioritasking' tool is a great time-management tool to help you prioritise tasks on the basis of urgency and importance.

It is a prioritisation matrix that highlights four quadrants within which you can prioritise tasks and demands, and thereby better manage your time.

---

[25] Brian Tracy, *Eat that Frog!*, Berrett-Koehler, 2001

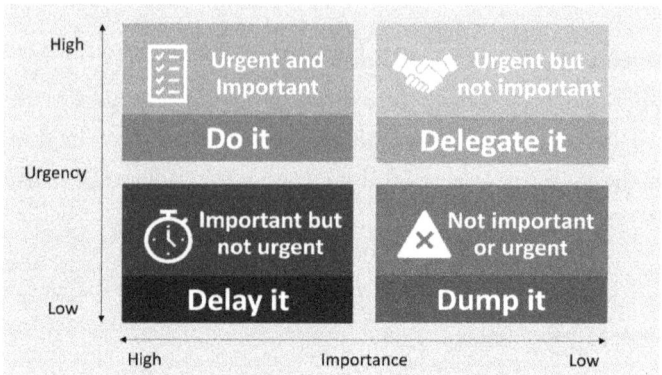

FIGURE 14:   The 4 D's of Prioritasking

The manner in which you prioritise demands to reduce stress works like this:

-> If a demand is of high urgency and high importance, you Do It.

-> If a demand is of high urgency but low importance, you Delegate It.

-> If a demand is of high importance but low urgency, you Delay It.

-> If a demand is of low importance and low urgency, you Dump It.

Below are some examples of actionable items that you can prioritask and be more effective at work.

#1: Do It

These work tasks are urgent and important. They require your immediate attention:

DO IT	EXAMPLES
Emergencies, complaints, crisis issues.	- Handling a sudden system breakdown. - Addressing customer complaints. - Managing a security breach.
Demands from superiors or customers.	- Urgent requests from your manager. - High-priority customer orders. - Immediate client inquiries.
Planned tasks or project work now due.	- Meeting project milestones / deadlines. - Completing project-related tasks on time.
Meetings and appointments.	- Attending critical client meetings. - Staff reviews and team discussions. - Important project-related meetings.
Reports and other submissions.	- Preparing and submitting reports. - Compliance reporting. - Submitting a project proposal.
Staff issues or needs.	- Handling staff's urgent matters. - Assisting with staff-related difficulties.
Problem resolution, fire-fighting, fixes.	- Troubleshooting system issues. - Addressing security vulnerabilities. - Fixing production line problems.

TABLE 9:   Urgent & Important Tasks – Do It

Confirm the importance and the urgency of these tasks, then do them now.

> Tip: Prioritise according to relative urgency. You can even use the $25,000 Idea and itemise these tasks accordingly.

#2: Delay It

These tasks are not urgent but they are important. They require you to diarise or delay them:

DELAY IT	EXAMPLES
Planning, preparation, scheduling.	- Setting up meetings and appointments. - Creating weekly schedules or plans. - Scheduling regular training sessions.
Research, investigation, designing, testing.	- Conducting in-depth market research. - Investigating technical issues or opportunities. - Designing templates for reports.
Networking relationship building.	- Engaging in frequent networking events. - Building professional relationships. - Attending industry conferences.
Thinking, creating, designing.	- Brainstorming ideas for innovation. - Creating materials for presentations. - Modelling process improvements.
Systems and process development.	- Developing new workflow systems. - Creating process improvement plans. - Project management templates.
Anticipation and prevention.	- Risk assessment and management. - Identifying issues before they occur. - Developing contingency plans.
Developing change, direction, strategy.	- Crafting long-term business strategies. - Planning change initiatives. - Establishing new corporate directions.

TABLE 10: Not Urgent but Important Tasks – Delay It

The skillsets critical to the success of tasks in this quadrant are: planning, strategic thinking, deciding direction and aims.

Tip: Plan time and personal space for these tasks.

#3: Delegate It

These tasks are urgent but they are not important. They require you to delegate them, or to 'reject and explain':

DELEGATE IT	EXAMPLES
Trivial requests from others.	- Answering non-urgent emails or calls. - Attending to unimportant requests. - Handling minor administrative tasks.
Apparent emergencies.	- Addressing situations falsely perceived as crises or minor incidents that appear as emergencies.
Ad-hoc interruptions and distractions.	- Managing interruptions in your work. - Attending to non-essential distractions. - Unproductive meetings / conversations.
Mis-understandings appearing as complaints.	- Resolving minor conflicts, disputes, or complaints that arise from insignificant issues or misunderstandings. - Dealing with grievances that are not critical to the organisation.
Pointless routines or activities.	- Following mundane, repetitive procedures or tasks. - Engaging in activities that don't contribute significantly to goals. - Carrying out trivial tasks that can be automated or simplified.

Accumulated unresolved trivia.	- Clearing out a backlog of low-priority tasks and issues - Addressing small matters that have piled up over time. - Handling miscellaneous and unimportant responsibilities.
Boss's whims or tantrums.	- Managing demands or requests from superiors that lack importance. - Handling the whims or unpredictable reactions of a supervisor. - Attending to requests or directions from a boss with low significance.

TABLE 11: Urgent but Not Important Tasks – Delegate It

The skillset critical to the success of tasks in this quadrant is to scrutinise and probe the demands placed on you.

> Tip: Help others to re-assess their requests, and wherever possible reject and avoid these tasks (see *Strategies for Effectively Saying 'No'*).

#4: Dump It

These tasks are not urgent and are not important. They require you to dump them:

DUMP IT	EXAMPLES
'Comfort' activities.	- Leisure activities during work hours. - Computer games or internet surfing. - Frequent and extended cigarette breaks.
Socialising.	- Non-work-related chats and gossip. - Spending excessive time on social media and unrelated conversations. - Procrastinating through socialising.
Disengagement.	- Daydreaming or mind-wandering. - Doodling or non-productive activities. - Over-extended breaks without reason.
Irrelevant reading material.	- Reading content or materials that has no relevance to your tasks or work (such as unrelated articles, books, websites). - Consuming information with no connection to your job or responsibilities.
Unnecessary tinkering.	- Tinkering with equipment or tools that do not require attention. - Tweaking settings, objects, or processes that have no meaningful impact on work. - Engaging in actions that waste time in minor equipment modifications.
Embellishment and over-production.	- Unnecessary extra work beyond required standards. - Over-producing documents, reports, or work output beyond what is necessary. - Time spent on non-essential details that don't contribute significantly to goals.

TABLE 12:   Not Urgent and Not Important Tasks – Dump It

These tasks are not true tasks. They are non-productive, de-motivational, and tiresome.

The skillset critical to 'tasks' in this quadrant is to minimise or cease them altogether.

Tip: Even better, plan to avoid them at all costs.

Using the prioritasking matrix, here are some questions to consider when prioritasking the things you need to do:

Q: What are 4 tasks you can prioritask in your personal life right now?

1. Do It?
2. Delay It?
3. Delegate It?
4. Dump It?

Q: What are 4 tasks you can prioritask in your work right now?

1. Do It?
2. Delay It?
3. Delegate It?
4. Dump It?

Batching

Batching similar tasks like phone calls, meetings, coffee 'catch ups', and emails is also an efficient time-management strategy.

For instance, I try to batch all my meetings on a Thursday

afternoon at the same location, if possible, so that I minimise time travelling to and from meeting points and minimise waiting times to meet clients.

This strategy alone can save me 4-5 hours per week.

> Q: What are some tasks you can batch together in your personal life right now?

> Q: What are some tasks you can batch together in your work right now?

E: EXCLUDE NON-ESSENTIALS

The fourth time-management strategy, *Exclude Non-Essentials*, includes:

1. Blocking out time when you're *not* available to complete important tasks.

2. Focus on one task and eliminate distractions (for example, emails, social media).

3. 20-30 minutes per day of *uni-tasking* to reduce half-work and incompletions.

4. End your workday.

Block Out Time

The recent shift to increasing numbers of staff working remotely from home brings great advantages and flexibility. You don't need to waste hundreds of hours per year commuting to and from work.

You can work during hours that best suit your natural daily rhythms and family commitments. You don't even have to get out of your pyjamas!

But there is also a downside: *distraction*.

It is much easier to get distracted in the home with household chores that need doing: washing dishes, ironing, dusting, vacuuming the floors, and other things. Not to mention the kids at home who like to interrupt your important online meetings.

Even in the workplace there are distractions: conversations that filter to you, emails that pop up while you're at your desk computer, colleagues that interrupt, and bosses that demand your immediate attention.

A great solution to minimise distraction and interruptions is to block out periods of time (for example, 30-60 minutes) when you're *not* available so that you can complete important tasks.

> Q: What times during the day can you block out when you're *not* available so you can focus on important tasks?

Eliminate Distractions

Another approach to exclude non-essentials is to eliminate distractions like email and social media. You can do this by:

> -> Turning off social media and/or email notifications on your mobile device or computer.

-> Allocating specific 'social media' time during the day when you will only catch up on your social media posts during that allocated period of time.

-> Set specific times aside to answer emails (for example, morning, last thing in the afternoon) and/or do your online shopping.

Tip: The 'Time Audit' is a great tool to help you understand and identify how much time you waste on social media, TV, and other distractions during your day.

Q: When is the best time to set aside for:

1. Social Media?

2. eMails?

3. Online Shopping/Web Browsing?

Uni-tasking

Most people have heard of multi-tasking, but how many have heard of uni-tasking?

Uni-tasking is the opposite of multi-tasking, whereby you focus only on one task at a time and not several. It is an efficient time-management strategy to help exclude non-essentials. It also ties in with the time-management strategy of *Itemise the Day*.

Setting aside 20-30 minutes each day to uni-task is a great way to finish those half-finished or uncompleted tasks that are lingering on your desk.

William James was an American philosopher in the mid-19th Century and is considered the father of American psychology. He is the author of several books, including *The Varieties of Religious Experience*.[26] James made this statement about human nature to let things remain half-completed:

> *Nothing is so fatiguing as the eternal hanging on of an uncompleted task.*

Uni-tasking is a simple strategy to help you improve the habit of completion. As one attendee at my workshops said, "Uni-tasking is easy wins."

Uni-tasking is like picking low-hanging fruit. It's an easy way to get things completed and get through your to-do list.

> Q: What are three half-completed tasks that you can 'uni-task' at home or in your personal life?

> Q: What are three half-completed tasks that you can 'uni-task' at work?

End Your Workday

In our discussion on *Consequences of Not Saying 'No'*, we discussed that a healthy work-life balance is essential for overall personal development and well-being, and that an inability to say 'no' can lead to excessive overtime and/or bringing work home after hours and on the weekends.

---

[26] *The Varieties of Religious Experience: A Study of Human Nature*, William James, Oxford University Press, 2012 (first published 1902)

So the last step in excluding non-essentials is to end your workday.

Do you regularly bring work home that could easily remain at the office? Do you stay up late working on projects or tasks that should be done during work hours? Are your weekends yours or do you still do work?

Sometimes it isn't practical to end the workday immediately. Important projects and deadlines sometimes need to be met. But these are more often the exception, not the rule.

If you're constantly bringing your work home, ask yourself:

1. Could I improve my efficiency during my work hours so that I don't have to bring work home?

2. Are there others at work who could help me complete my tasks on time?

3. Having self-initiative and going the extra mile is important, but am I bringing work home to impress my boss or others? Do they actually notice all the extra work I'm doing at home?

M. Scott Peck was an American psychiatrist and author of the groundbreaking book, *The Road Less Traveled*.[27] He said:

> *Until you value yourself, you won't value your time. Until you value your time, you will not do anything with it.*

---

[27] M. Scott Peck, *The Road Less Traveled: A New Psychology of Love, Traditional Values and Spiritual Growth*, Arrow Books, 1978

If you are habitually bringing work home, understanding the reasons why you do will help you to manage your time and end your workday more regularly.

Your family will appreciate it and your physical and mental health will benefit too.

> Tip: The 'Time Audit' is a great tool to help you understand and identify how much time you spend after hours at home doing tasks that are best done at work.

TIME-MANAGEMENT TOOLS & TECHNIQUES

There are just as many tools for time-management as there are strategies, and there are a great many books on the subject of time-management and personal development that can help you, so we will only briefly mention some select tools and techniques.

Effectively managing your time requires the use of various planning tools, which can significantly enhance your productivity.

Here are some essential planning tools and tips to integrate into your time-management routine:

Daily To-Do Lists:

These lists help you prioritise tasks for the day, ensuring that you focus on what's most important. Be realistic about what you can accomplish in a day and avoid overwhelming yourself with too many tasks.

Master Lists:

Master lists serve as repositories for all your tasks and goals. You can categorise them, such as your 7 Life Segments, and use them as references when creating daily to-do lists.

Planners (Daily, Weekly, Monthly, Yearly):

Planners provide a structured way to organise your time. They are available in various formats, including digital, electronic, or physical, like paper planners or diaries. Whatever your preference, it's important to incorporate the use of these tools in all your 7 Life Segments.

End-of-Day Planning:

Spend a few minutes at the end of each day to plan for the next. Review your accomplishments and set clear goals for the following day. This practice allows you to start your day with purpose and direction.

Start-of-Week Planning:

At the beginning of each week, look ahead to identify key tasks and priorities. Plan your schedule to ensure you allocate time to important projects and commitments.

Start-of-Month Planning:

Monthly planning provides a broader view of your goals and objectives. It's an opportunity to set priorities for the month, align tasks with your long-term objectives, and make necessary adjustments.

Tip: While planning is essential, it's important to allow flexibility in your schedule. Unexpected events or opportunities may arise, and rigid planning can lead to stress. Adaptability is key.

The importance of using these time-management tools, like planners and to-do lists, is to provide organisation and structure in your daily life. They help you maintain clarity about your goals, minimise distractions, and help you to use your time efficiently.

With effective planning, you can accomplish tasks more systematically and make room for other important aspects of your life, such as personal well-being, creativity, and relaxation.

When used well and with discipline, these tools can help you maximise your personal and professional effectiveness.

If it's not scheduled, it won't get done.

Main Points:

1. Time-management isn't just about clock-watching or creating endless to-do lists; it's a fundamental skill that enables you to maximise your productivity, reduce stress, tackle unforeseen challenges, seize opportunities, and achieve your goals with greater efficiency.

2. Time is the only thing we can't afford to lose.

3. Good time-management is about good self-management.

4. Effective time-managers know where their time goes. They don't have a vague idea. They know exactly, and they actively work on eliminating their time-stealers and time-wasters.

5. A time audit helps you identify your time-stealers and time-wasters.

6. Itemising your day is the $25,000 idea— the idea of taking things one at a time in their proper order.

7. Successful tasks make successful days. Successful days build a successful life.

8. Prioritasking helps you to identify the most important and urgent things you need to do first.

9. Uni-task to finish uncompleted tasks that are lingering on your desk and reduce the habit of half-work.

10. If it's not scheduled, it won't get done.

14 EFFECTIVE GOAL-SETTING

'You are never too old to set another goal or to dream a new dream.'

C.S. Lewis

YOUR CAPABILITY AND capacity is greatly enhanced with effective energy-management and effective time-management.

So too with effective goal-setting. When done right, goal-setting will increase your capability to do more than you ever thought you could, as well as increase your capacity to do more.

Goal-setting is a well-known strategy for boosting the chances of achieving your objectives. Businesses do it. Government departments do it. Entrepreneurs do it. Educational institutions do it. Financial planners do it. Personal trainers do it.

So the question is: Do you do it?

There is a bank of research to show that those who write down their goals are far more likely to turn their dreams into reality. Which is why I actively advise my clients to set goals in their 7 Life Segments using my '4 STAR Rules' of goal-setting:

-> **S:** Set Own Goals.

-> **T:** Think on Paper.

-> **A:** Apply Yourself (Be Committed).

-> **R:** Responsibility (Be Accountable).

S: Set Own Goals

Begin by establishing clear, well-defined goals that reflect your desires and objectives in all your 7 Life Segments. Define what you want to achieve in each segment, and be as specific as possible.

T: Think on Paper

Transcribing your thoughts into written words not only makes your goals more tangible but also engages your mind in a deeper and more meaningful way. Writing down your goals clarifies your intentions and what you want to achieve, as well as solidifying your commitment to your goals.

A: Apply Yourself (Be Committed)

Your goals are more likely to be achieved when you are committed to the pursuit of your goals. This means applying yourself. Effective goal-setting is not just about writing them down; it's about actively working toward them. Your application and commitment drives your actions.

R: Responsibility (Be Accountable)

Accept responsibility for your actions and progress because when you encounter setbacks or face challenges, the act of accountability keeps you on track. You are answerable to yourself, which serves as a powerful motivator to keep pushing forward to the achievement of your goals.

We will now discuss these 4 STAR Rules of effective goal-setting in more detail.

S: SET OWN GOALS

There are many great books on how to set goals, so without wanting to repeat what's already available for you, I'm just going to highlight the important elements of goal-setting.

In the game of soccer, scoring an own goal is a severe blunder. It's hard enough to score a goal for your own team, but to hand the opposition a gift makes winning so much more difficult.

Yet I say,

The best goals are own goals.

The goals that you set for your own personal and professional life, of course: individual goals, relationship goals, career goals.

In your journey through life, some of the most valuable goals you can set are the ones that come from within—your personal and professional aspirations, the dreams you harbour for yourself and the people around you, the objectives that propel your career forward.

These are the goals that resonate at the core of your being. When you set personal goals, you embark on a path of self-discovery and self-fulfillment. These goals are intrinsically linked to your values, desires, and purpose.

> *By defining your own goals, you take charge of your destiny, paving the way for personal growth and success on your terms.*

In regards to your own personal goals, you might set goals related to your health, well-being, personal development, or even your hobbies and interests. These goals are not imposed upon you; they emerge from your own heart and mind.

Whether it's a commitment to leading a healthier lifestyle, mastering a new skill, or exploring your creative passions, personal goals have the power to enrich your life in countless ways.

Relationship goals hold immense importance as well. These objectives focus on nurturing and strengthening the bonds you share with your loved ones. They involve promoting healthier communication, deepening emotional connections, and creating a more harmonious and loving environment for your family and friends.

Relationship goals are deeply personal, reflecting your values and your desire to cultivate meaningful connections with those you care about most.

When it comes to career goals, you are in fact planning a path towards your own professional aspirations. Whether you're seeking advancement in your current job, exploring new career opportunities, or even considering entrepreneurship, these goals align with your ambitions and the direction you envision for your career.

These goals empower you to take control of your professional life, driving you to excel and achieve the success you desire.

The key to setting goals effectively lies in one word: balance.

It's essential to set goals that balance the various aspects of your 7 Life Segments, like personal, professional, and financial goals.

While financial success is undoubtedly important, an excessive focus on material gain at the expense of other aspects of your life can lead to disillusionment.

Of course, achieving financial stability and enjoying the fruits of your labour are worthy objectives, but it's equally crucial to remember that life is multi-dimensional.

The pursuit of personal growth, meaningful relationships, and a fulfilling career should coexist with your financial aspirations. This balance ensures that you create a well-rounded and meaningful life, where you're not just accumulating wealth but also experiencing personal and professional fulfillment.

> *The best reason to set own goals is not as destinations to arrive at, but as the means by which you grow into the person you always wanted to be and always thought you could.*

In essence, the best goals are the ones that spring from your own aspirations and values. These goals provide a sense of purpose, motivation, and direction, each playing a vital role in shaping a rewarding and meaningful life.

So, set your goals with self-awareness, balance, and the understanding that your own goals are the most significant milestones in your life's wonderful journey.

Q: What are three goals that you would like to achieve in each of your 7 Life Segments within the next 12 months?

-> Family & Relationships?

-> Career & Work?

-> Money & Finances?

-> Health & Wellbeing?

-> Learning & Education?

-> Fun & Adventure?

-> Spirituality & Ethics?

Q: What are three goals that you would like to achieve in each of your 7 Life Segments within the next 5 years?

Q: What are three goals that you would like to achieve in each of your 7 Life Segments within your lifetime?

T: THINK ON PAPER

Because of the incredible power of committing your goals to paper, international speaker and author, Brian Tracy, says we should all 'think on paper'.

The impact of the written word on human motivation and achievement is undeniable. There is power in the written word, and the act of writing down your own goals serves as a catalyst for your success.

Setting and achieving goals is a multifaceted neurological process that engages both the creative and logical aspects of your brain. Harmonising your imaginative right brain with your analytical left brain is vital for effective goal-setting and goal-getting, a process that I call '100% Goal Setting'.

Your right brain is a creative powerhouse, responsible for envisioning your future and painting a mental picture of what you want to achieve.

> *Your right brain is where all your possibilities, dreams, and desires are first imagined. It's where you generate ideas, desires, and aspirations.*

When you imagine your future, your right brain is in action, creating the vision that you want for yourself. This is the emotional, imaginative part of goal setting, where you tap into your deepest desires and dreams.

On the other hand, your left brain is the rational, logical thinker that breaks down your vision into actionable steps. It's the part of your brain that is responsible for organisation, planning, and problem-solving.

This is where you devise strategies, create plans, and work out the detailed steps required to make your goals a reality. It's the pragmatic side of goal-setting, where you figure out how to bridge the gap between where you are now and where you want to be.

Now, here's the crux of the matter:

> *If you merely hold your goals within your mind's eye without committing them to paper, you're effectively limiting yourself to using just one half of your brain.*

If you don't write down your goals, you're only engaging your creative right brain while neglecting the left brain's critical role in planning and execution.

However, when you write down your goals on paper, you activate your entire brain. This is '100% Goal Setting', which taps into your creative imagination and logical reasoning.

Writing down your goals makes them tangible, creating a bridge between your dreams and the actionable steps needed to realise them. By doing this, you're not just visualising your goals, you're transforming them into a structured plan, making your objectives more concrete and achievable.

> *'100% Goal Setting' maximises your chances of completing your goals. Your right brain gives birth to the vision, and your left brain formulates the roadmap to that vision.*

Goal-setting, therefore, isn't just a matter of dreaming; it's about bridging the dream with reality through action. When you employ your whole brain by writing down your goals, you embrace the full spectrum of your ingenuity.

Daring to Dream... Your Want List

Your right brain is your creative brain. So to activate this part of your brain, I would like you to now consider an exercise called, 'Daring to Dream'.

Think about the things—experiences, states of being, places, relationships, and so forth—you *really* want in your 7 Life Segments. Although there are probably a thousand things that you know you don't want, it's equally vital that you also know, and have great clarity about, the things you *do* want in life.

When you do this exercise, remember that the value of your effectiveness is directly proportional to your desire to help other people (see our discussion on *Effective Value*).

Helping others is the key to success and happiness. The happiest people in life, therefore, are those who set collaborative goals, not competitive goals. That is, goals that are win-win.

> Q: Make your 'Daring to Dream' list here:
>
> I *really* want...
>
> I *really* want...
>
> I *really* want...
>
> I *really* want...
>
> I *really* want...
>
> I *really* want...
>
> I *really* want...
>
> I *really* want...
>
> I *really* want...
>
> I *really* want...

A: APPLY YOURSELF

Another benefit of writing down your goals is that it sets commitment. The act of transcribing your aspirations into written words means your commitment is no longer a fleeting thought; it's a documented statement to yourself that you can revisit as often as needed.

This commitment is a powerful motivator. It solidifies your determination to take action and work diligently toward your goals.

Whenever you revisit your written goals, you reinforce your commitment, which in turn strengthens your resolve to persevere, especially when faced with obstacles and challenges.

In moments of doubt or when you encounter setbacks, your written goals remind you of your commitment and they reinforce your desire to strive for your dreams. This commitment provides you with the necessary emotional and mental energy to keep moving forward no matter what.

Some goals, however, are so big they are overwhelming. No matter how committed you are, they are so big they can frighten you into inaction. They are so de-motivating they cause you to give up and stop.

This is where writing your goals down can help you move past the overwhelm, yet another benefit of '100% Goal Setting'.

Goals are more likely to become a reality when they are broken down to small steps or actions that you can incorporate into your everyday activities.

Breaking your goals down into manageable, bite-sized chunks is the answer to the question of how do you eat an elephant?

Let's use the example of writing a novel. A good-sized novel is about 100,000 words, which can be a bit overwhelming. But if I write 1,000 words per week, which is not overwhelming, I will be able to finish my novel in 100 weeks, or about two years.

Now, that might be a bit too long for me. So I'll aim for 2,000 words per week, which is still doable. This will mean I will finish the book in 50 weeks, or about 1 year.

Again, that time frame might be a bit too long for me. So I'll aim for 4,000 words per week, which I can still comfortably do, and aim to finish my novel in about 25 weeks, or about six months.

I can break this down even further by writing 800 words a day for five days of the week. This leaves two days free to do other things, or to have as a buffer should something unforeseen happen and I am unable to complete my word count goals on my assigned writing days.

This seems feasible and realistic.

> -> Goal = 100,000-word novel.

> -> Breakdown = 800 words per day, five days a week, is realistic and achievable.

> -> Time-frame = A deadline of six months to complete my novel.

Other goals that you can set using this breakdown method include:

- Saving for a home loan deposit or holiday.
- Weight loss.
- Exercise and fitness.
- Learning a musical instrument or a new language.

Q: Action plan the goals you would like to achieve in your 7 Life Segments:

-> 5/3/1 year:

-> 6 months:

-> 3 months:

-> 1 month:

-> 7-days:

-> Daily:

R: RESPONSIBILITY

Another benefit of goal-setting and writing them down is that your accountability is bolstered. When your goals are written on paper, there's a sense of responsibility that naturally arises. You're more likely to follow through because you've documented your intentions.

Accountability is a key component of being effective, but it is often overlooked. You can either be accountable to yourself (that is, take responsibility for your thoughts, emotions, and behaviours), or you can have an accountability partner to hold you accountable to do the things you say you will do.

Being held accountable to yourself or by another is a great incentive to keep working toward your goal. Because when you are held accountable, you are less likely to procrastinate and more likely to take the action you need to take.

Bob Proctor, motivational speaker and international bestselling author of *You Were Born Rich*,[28] said this about the power of accountability:

> *Accountability is the glue that ties commitment to results.*

Accountability stems from the word 'account', which means to tally up, to keep score. This underlies the power of effective goal-setting. Thinking on paper and breaking down your goals helps you to 'keep score' of the things you need to do to achieve your vision.

The impact is especially so when goals are written down and visible. For example, pinned to a corkboard at or near your main place of work—it's very hard to ignore goals that you see and review every day.

> Q: Who can be an accountability partner to help you reach your personal or professional goals and be more effective?

> Q: How often will you check in with your accountability partner?

---

[28] Bob Proctor, *You Were Born Rich: Now You Can Discover And Develop Those Riches*, LifeSuccess Productions, 1997

Main Points:

1. The best reason to set own goals is not as destinations to arrive at, but as the means by which you grow into the person you always wanted to be and always thought you could.

2. There is power in the written word, and the act of writing down your goals serves as a catalyst for your success.

3. '100% Goal Setting' maximises your chances of completing your goals. Your right brain gives birth to the vision, and your left brain formulates the roadmap to that vision.

4. Do you dare to dream?

5. Goals are more likely to become a reality when they are broken down to small steps or actions that you can incorporate into your everyday activities.

6. Accountability is the glue that ties commitment to results.

HOW IT ALL WORKS

'Commitment is an act, not a word.'
Jean-Paul Sartre

WE HAVE NOW come full circle. Along the way, we've journeyed through the realm of personal and professional effectiveness.

We've discovered the fundamental equation for success:

$$E = MC^2$$

Where E is your effectiveness, and M is your mindset, C_1 is your capability, and C_2 is your capacity.

Our exploration began by understanding how your mindset shapes your effectiveness, paving the way for self-awareness and self-empowerment. With the right mindset, you've harnessed the ability to unlock your potential and overcome life's challenges.

We then delved into capability and capacity. Your capability represents your power to accomplish tasks, while your capacity signifies the volume of physical, mental, and emotional 'space' you can hold. Boosting these factors has a profound impact on your effectiveness.

But at the core of our discussion, we've uncovered the driving force behind it all—*choice*.

Your choices dictate whether you enhance your mindset, capability, and capacity, or restrict them. The choices you make today, and those you will make in the future, are the key to your transformation.

Remember, your current effectiveness is a direct result of the choices you've made in the past, and your future effectiveness lies in the choices you have yet to make.

Effectiveness is, at its heart, about choice.

Effective self-leadership is therefore about making better choices. It's about recognising the critical link between our thoughts (choices) and the reality we experience. What we place our attention on significantly influences our lives.

With our thoughts (choices), we create our circus.

As we conclude, I encourage you to recognise the incredible power of your choices. Embrace the opportunities for personal growth, expand your horizons, and create a life of purpose, meaning, and effectiveness.

Create a life of no limits, and escape the flea circus.

THE POWER OF COMMITMENT

Remember in the introduction of this guidebook when you were asked what areas of the Life Leadership Compass you needed to work on and strengthen?

> Q: How does it compare with your current self-leadership now?

> Q: What level of effectiveness do you believe you can realistically achieve following The Effectiveness Equation—$E = MC^2$?

This level can now be your 'effectiveness' goal, but bear in mind that any success requires long-term commitment, and effective self-leadership is no different.

> *...until one is committed there is hesitancy, the chance to draw back, always ineffectiveness. Concerning all acts of initiative (and creation), there is one elementary truth, the ignorance of which kills countless ideas and splendid plans: that the moment one definitely commits oneself then providence moves too... All sorts of things occur to help one that would never otherwise have occurred. A whole stream of events issues from the decision, raising in one's favour all manner of unforeseen incidents and meetings and material assistance, which no man could have dreamt would have come his way.*

W.H. Murray. The Scottish Himalayan Expedition, 1951

I now offer you a contract with yourself to commit to the principles of self-leadership outlined in this guidebook:

Contractual Agreement:

On this date_____

I _____

do hereby commit to the principles of *The Effectiveness Equation: $E = MC^2$* in order to fulfil my goal of being more effective and function at my optimal ability.

I recognise that the power to be more effective is in my hands and nobody else. I recognise the importance of the process of self-leadership, and I recognise that the process of personal effectiveness is a process that never ends.

I hereby make this lifelong commitment to myself.

Signed: _____

90-DAY CHALLENGE

Now that you've signed a contract with yourself to commit to the principles of The Effectiveness Equation, I offer one last challenge to you.

After 90 days of putting into practice the techniques of self-leadership outlined in this book, you will notice a significant, long-term improvement in your everyday effectiveness.

If you feel that you have failed to achieve your 'effectiveness' goals, after honestly applying the principles of The Effectiveness Equation, then please contact me and I will offer you free enrolment in any one of the Life Leadership workshops, seminars, or courses of your choice. Or you can choose a free copy of any of my available books from DoctorZed Publishing.

It can't be more stress-free than that!

If the content of this guidebook contributes to your ability to increase your personal and professional effectiveness, I am delighted to have had some positive impact and I am grateful for the opportunity to help.

If you would like to learn more about my Life Leadership programs, I'd be honoured to help you further. I have devoted myself to making the world a better place by helping others fulfil their immense potential and to make themselves better people.

Dr. Scott Zarcinas

Connect with DoctorZed

Facebook: YNSOB.by.Dr.Scott.Zarcinas
LinkedIn: dr-scott-zarcinas-6572399
Instagram: doctorzed_motivational_speaker
Twitter: @DrScottZarcinas
Website: *scottzarcinas.com*

Growing great people is how you grow a great business!

Are you a leader of a team, involved in a team environment, a business owner, or entrepreneur looking to grow your business?

Ask me how I can help your business grow by growing your people.

E: scott.zarcinas@doctorzed.com
W: scottzarcinas.com/contact

The Life You Want, the Way You Want, How You Want!

Looking for a coach or mentor to help you get direction and take your life to the next level?

Ask me how I can help you maximise your capabilities and reach your fullest potential.

E: scott.zarcinas@doctorzed.com
W: scottzarcinas.com/contact

Book DoctorZed for Your Next Function!
Keynotes • MC • Presentations

scottzarcinas.com/book-doctorzed/

Other Titles by Scott Zarcinas

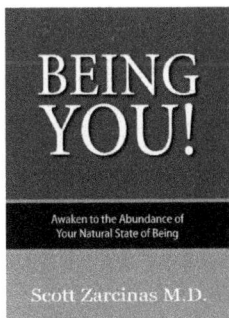

Being YOU! Awaken to the Abundance of Your Natural State of Being
by Scott Zarcinas M.D.
ISBN: 978-0-6456384-8-6
eISBN: 978-0-6456384-9-3
DoctorZed Publishing

Available in print and ebook.

'Refreshing. A tonic to read. Comprehensive and scholarly, it also has so many poetic qualities.'
~ Roger Rees, Emeritus Professor of Disability Studies and Research, Flinders University

You already have what you are looking for!

Ever wanted the answers to life's deepest questions: Who am I? Why do I do what I do? What am I doing with my life?

When you awaken to the abundance of your natural state of being, you will get to the heart of the motivating forces and innermost needs of your life.

But unlike 'quick fix' and 'step-by-step' guides, this book offers real solutions to living a life of abundance through the understanding of your true self.

www.scottzarcinas.com/books/being-you

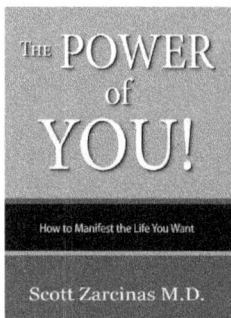

The Power of YOU! How to Manifest the Life You Want
by Scott Zarcinas M.D.

ISBN: 978-06456384-5-5

eISBN: 978-06456384-6-2

DoctorZed Publishing

Available in print and ebook.

Featuring 4 Power Habits of Success

For every 20 babies that are born, only one of them will be deemed 'successful' at the age of 65—only 5% of the population.

But those in The 5% Club are no different from anyone else. They have just learned the secret of success, which you can too.

The secret is this: Success is merely a habit. When you get your habits right, your membership to The 5% Club is guaranteed.

This book is your go-to manual if:

• You need to get off the hamster wheel and start living.

• You want to thrive, not just survive.

• You seek the know-how to manifest the life you want.

www.scottzarcinas.com/books/the-power-of-you

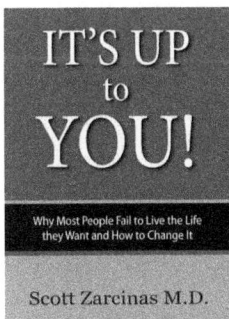

It's Up to YOU! Why Most People Fail to Live the Life they Want and How to Change It
by Scott Zarcinas M.D.
ISBN: 978-06485726-5-7
eISBN: 978-06485726-3-3
DoctorZed Publishing

Available in print and ebook.

Featuring 9 Life Leadership Strategies to Live the Life You Want, the Way You Want, How You Want.

Do you feel stuck in a rut? Is your life on hold? Are you looking for new direction but don't know which way to turn?

We all want to do more than just survive; we want to thrive. But if you're trapped in the same old routine, now is the time to start living the life you were born to live—with abundance.

This book is your go-to manual if:

• You need a break from the old and to take a new direction.

• You desire greater success and fulfillment.

• You seek the confidence to be yourself and not what others expect you to be.

www.scottzarcinas.com/books/its-up-to-you

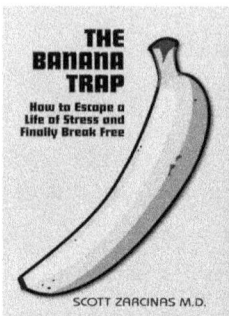

The Banana Trap: How to Escape a Life of Stress and Finally Break Free
by Scott Zarcinas M.D.
ISBN: 978-0-6485726-1-9
eISBN: 978-0-6487107-9-0
DoctorZed Publishing

Available in print and ebook.

*Science-based Stress Management
Strategies to De-Stress & Prosper*

Do you feel overwhelmed and over-stressed? Are you trapped in recurring cycles of worry and frustration? Do you crumble in stressful moments?

Don't worry, everybody has moments of high stress and overwhelm! This guidebook will help you to:

- Feel less overwhelmed and more confident.
- Escape The Banana Trap and reclaim your life.
- Identify and overcome the different types of stress.
- Eliminate stressful habits and increase happiness.
- Deal with high-pressure situations and be in control.

PLUS develop a long-term strategy to prevent high stress before it occurs.

www.scottzarcinas.com/books/the-banana-trap

www.ingramcontent.com/pod-product-compliance
Lightning Source LLC
Chambersburg PA
CBHW030912090426
42737CB00007B/167